What People are Saying about
Take Someone with You to Heaven

"Like many others who have gone into prisons and jails with us, Chuck and Carol Middlekauff demonstrate what our ministry is all about. We train Christian 'teammates' to share the good news and love of Christ with 'the least of these' so they can continue to do it with others they encounter as they go along. In this book, Carol has written the stories of some of those encounters so you can appreciate how easy it is to tell people about Jesus. It happens when you realize God does all the work, and all you have to do is show up. I hope you will be encouraged by reading the book and then join us soon for a Weekend of Champions to find out for yourself."

Bill Glass, retired NFL all-pro defensive end, evangelist, founder of Bill Glass Champions for Life prison ministries, and author of numerous books, including _The Healing Power of a Father's Blessing_ and _Blitzed by Blessings_

"Since you became a Christian, have you wanted to share your faith but always chickened out? Almost a hundred percent of believers would have to answer 'Yes' to that question. But if your answer is yes, how can you call yourself a Christian? How can you go to church and claim to be worshipping God when you have been rebellious to Jesus' Great Commission, when you have refused to follow Jesus' commandment every day of your life? If you want to stop living as a mediocre Christian, I pray for you as Paul prayed for Philemon, _I thank my God, making mention of you always in my prayers . . . that the sharing of your faith may become effective by the acknowledgement of every good thing which is in you in Christ Jesus_ (Philemon 6:6 NKJV).

"I have shared my faith, one-on-one, well over 10,000 times. It's not scary because it's not up to me. I have never led anyone to Christ. But I have been there many times when the Holy Spirit has done it. Now it's your turn. If you have been chicken to share your faith so far, this book will encourage you to stop your sin of silence and start enjoying a new fullness in Christ, experiencing the joy that comes from truly following Him."

Bill Fay, Evangelist and author of _Share Jesus without Fear_

"I had the privilege of pastoring Carol Middlekauff for six years while serving as pastor of Great Hills Baptist Church in Austin, Texas from 2003 to 2009, and I can honestly say that Carol is a testimony of what God can and will do with a person who is fully surrendered to the calling of the Lord Jesus to be a soul-winner. Carol genuinely walks with the Lord, and she has a consuming passion to share the gospel with every person she meets. Her writings will bless, inspire, and challenge you to see God at work around you saving souls and to join Him by delivering the message of the gospel. My heart overflows with gratitude for how Carol and her husband Chuck exemplify a passion for sharing the gospel of Jesus Christ with as many people as they possibly can in their lifetime.

"Someone has well said, 'The gospel of Jesus Christ is only good news if people hear it in time.' You will find in the pages of this book the passion that Carol lives out every day of her life. Your heart will be set on fire with a holy passion for souls as you read story after story of how God uses a faithful, available, intentional witness for His glory."
Dr. Michael S. Lewis, Executive Director, North American Missions Board

"Anyone can share their faith with others. That's the message Carol Middlekauff delivers in her account of the many divine appointments God has given her. You will be encouraged by her real-life stories and motivated by her challenge. Make yourself available and discover the joy of joining God in the great work of introducing others to eternal life, abundant and free."
John Sorensen, President, Evangelism Explosion International

Take Someone with You to Heaven

WestBow Press books may be ordered through booksellers or by contacting:

WestBow Press
A Division of Thomas Nelson
1663 Liberty Drive
Bloomington, IN 47403
www.westbowpress.com
1-(866) 928-1240

Because of the dynamic nature of the Internet, any web addresses or links contained in this book may have changed since publication and may no longer be valid. The views expressed in this work are solely those of the author and do not necessarily reflect the views of the publisher, and the publisher hereby disclaims any responsibility for them.

This book describes the author's and others' experiences of sharing the good news about Jesus. Some names and identifying details of individuals mentioned in the stories have been changed to protect their privacy. The quoted ideas expressed in this book (other than scriptures) are not exact quotations, but the author has attempted to maintain each speaker's original intent.

Scripture quotations marked NKJV are taken from the New King James Version®. Copyright © 1982 by Thomas Nelson, Inc. Used by permission. All rights reserved.

Scripture quotations marked NLT are taken from the Holy Bible, New Living Translation, copyright © 1996, 2004, 2007 by Tyndale House Foundation. Used by permission of Tyndale House Publishers, Inc., Carol Stream, Illinois 60188. All rights reserved.

Personal pronouns for God, Jesus, and the Holy Spirit (He, Him, Himself, His, etc.) are capitalized in the text and quoted scriptures, except those scriptures quoted directly from the New Living Translation (NLT).

Cover photo by Carol Middlekauff. Author photo by Cheryl Middlekauff

ISBN: 978-1-4497-8462-1 (sc)
ISBN: 978-1-4497-8461-4 (hc)
ISBN: 978-1-4497-8460-7 (e)

Library of Congress Control Number: 2013902442

Printed in the United States of America

WestBow Press rev. date: 3/19/2013

1 Christianity 2 Church 3 Ministry 4 Evangelism I. Title

To Jesus Christ who saved me, to the lost people of this world who need Jesus, and to the Christians who will lovingly share the good news of Jesus with them.

With thanks to evangelism trainers, Bill Fay, Bill Glass, Michael Lewis, Glenn Chappelear, and others; to friends, Laura Prado, Jesse Mullins, Dr. Zahea Nappa, and others for their encouragement and advice as I was writing this book; to my mother, Jean Hare, who has always championed my writing; and to my best friend and husband, Chuck, for his steadfast relationship with God, his enthusiasm for sharing the love and salvation of Jesus, and for loving me all these years.

Take Someone with You to Heaven

CAROL MIDDLEKAUFF

WESTBOW
PRESS
A DIVISION OF THOMAS NELSON

Contents

Preface

If you are *not 100 percent certain* where you would spend eternity if you died today, please begin this book by reading the gospel tract provided in Chapter 7.

If you are sure, I have written this book to show you how easy it is to share your faith. It's easy because God does all the work. You simply show up.

As you will read in the following chapters, watching God work as you become a part of His work is a joyful adventure. If you have a heart for Jesus, and you're willing, God is able.

The following stories are just a sampling of the glorious things God has done. And every week He does more. As you read, you will see I'm usually surprised, even stunned, at the way God's Word touches somebody when I speak up. You might think I've forgotten what He did the last time. Well, I know that God sets up divine appointments, but each situation is new and different, and as I go along encountering people, I can't imagine how God will do what He does—until He does it.

I always recognize my own shortcomings, and I sometimes get butterflies, wondering what I should do or say, or whether I should do or say anything. For that reason, I sometimes argue with the Holy Spirit, telling Him I'm not up to it—or just plain resisting. When I do speak up, beyond memorizing some scriptures and filling my mind with good Bible preaching, I don't have a plan about what I will say. But the Holy Spirit, as God promises in His word, always gives me the words. And when I obey His lead—whether I do it right away or after resisting—I always experience inexpressible joy. It will be the same for you.

You will be delivering the same good news, but every encounter will be unique. The most exciting times will be the unexpected meetings: the people who come up to you, the people God points out to you, people you don't expect to be interested in God but are.

The Holy Spirit doesn't give you everyone, but He does point out some people. It's important to be ready and willing when He does. It can happen anywhere, even, as you will read in Chapter 4, at a laundromat, or Chapter 5, in a New York deli, or Chapter 7, on an aisle at Walgreens. The opportunities will happen because you listen for the Holy Spirit's urgings, you truly care about people, and you take a little time to get involved with them.

Christ taught us that we must love all the people of the world—especially the lost people. So, when lost people behave badly, keep in mind that they are lost. That's how lost people act. As you encounter those lost people, remember the kind of love God had when He sent His only Son to die for you—and for them.

> Paul wrote: *But God demonstrates His own love toward us, in that while we were still sinners, Christ died for us.* (Romans 5:8 NKJV)

> In another message on love, Paul wrote: *And though I bestow all my goods to feed the poor, and though I give my body to be burned, but have not love, it profits me nothing.* (1 Corinthians 13:3 NKJV)

So, God loved you first. And love means a lot to Him. When you're sharing the love of God, the main thing to remember and demonstrate is the main thing: God's love.

Getting Started

Besides your own salvation experience, has anyone—outside church and not counting cussing—ever mentioned Jesus to you? Surveys show that—including pastors—only maybe five out of a hundred Christians have ever told anybody else what Jesus has done for them.

Here's the sad thing: The other ninety-five Christians are missing the joy of being there when someone receives God's gift of forgiveness (which is only available through trusting in Jesus), or when a prodigal person restores a broken relationship with Him, or when someone takes even a first tiny step in His direction. But *you* can have that joy.

Getting started is simple. Someone told me the good news about Jesus (the gospel message from the Bible). God led me to respond to it and filled me with the Holy Spirit. I'm going to heaven. And, through the power of the Holy Spirit, I'm taking a bunch of people with me.

I'm the most ordinary person you can imagine. My driver's license shows five feet tall, 110 pounds, chin-length gray hair, and an ordinary face with glasses. I've had no seminary studies and no speech coach. And considering the many definitions of "fool" in Proverbs, I think I qualify. What is extraordinary is that, when I show up, prayed up and ready to obey the Holy Spirit's lead, I have the thrill of watching God work—in me and through me. You can have it, too.

First, I started a relationship with Jesus when I was fifteen. Believing that I was a sinner, that He died to pay the penalty for my personal sins and then rose from the dead, I invited Him into my life. Then, after a prodigal time, when I strayed from God and came back, and then way too many years of sitting on the bench, mostly just praying, reading my Bible, and going to church, I finally committed my life to His Great Commission.

I asked Him to use me to share the gospel. And He has. It's been the very best time of my life. I hope you won't wait as long as I did.

Again, I'm an ordinary person. But I've told hundreds of people about Jesus, and I've passed out thousands of gospel tracts. Until I arrive in heaven, I won't know how many lives God changed after someone spent time with me on a front porch, parking lot, bus stop, or running trail, on a New York City street, or in a prison or jail, wanting to hear more about Jesus. And until I get to heaven, I won't know how many lives God will touch through those who took a tract—or found one in a trashcan, on the ground, or by a payphone. And I won't know how many lives God will change through this book. But please understand this: *God does all the work*. I can't brag about it. And you can't be afraid of it.

> *God has united you with Christ Jesus. For our benefit God made him to be wisdom itself. Christ made us right with God; he made us pure and holy, and he*

freed us from sin. Therefore, as the Scriptures say, "If you want to boast, boast only about the Lord." (1 Corinthians 1:30–31 NLT)

As you will read in these few stories, lots of people I've talked with have prayed with me to commit their lives to Jesus. Others were already Christians and found encouragement to rekindle their relationships with Jesus or to start introducing people to their Savior. And some folks I've encountered completely disagreed about the truth in God's Word. But they still wanted to talk about God, sometimes for hours.

Very, very few—maybe only one in hundreds—didn't want to talk about God at all. Those rare conversations usually ended abruptly. As you will read, a couple of those individuals even shouted at me. But I know they weren't rejecting me; they were rejecting Jesus. He loves them anyway. I figure He's working on them, or He wouldn't have sent me.

I repeat: very, very few didn't want to talk about God at all.

Life gives you things you have to do, things you want to do, and things you get to do. Sharing the hope of a Father in heaven who loves us and the promise of forgiveness in Jesus is one of those things you get to do.

You just have to start. You'll find out for yourself how much joy it brings. Like me, you will wonder why you didn't join God's harvest team sooner, why you didn't become a serious soldier in God's army when you were younger.

After all, no matter how many soldiers are on the battlefield, they will not win the battle unless someone marches forward when the commanding officer shouts "charge!" Have you heard God's order to charge—the Great Commission—but you are still just standing there?

To win this battle, someone has to march! If you're ready to start marching, I hope these stories will encourage you by showing you how simple it is to tell people about Jesus. I hope you are getting excited about seeing the extraordinary things that will happen when you do.

Even if you don't read every word of the stories, please take the time to read each scripture so the Holy Spirit can convict you and teach you to be a witness for Christ.

Also I heard the voice of the Lord, saying: "Whom shall I send, and who will go for Us?" Then I said, "Here am I! Send me." (Isaiah 6:8 NKJV)

In this scripture, God asked a question. Isaiah was the one who responded. Will you respond? _____

Chapter 1

The Great Commission

Jesus proclaims the Great Commission:

And Jesus came and spoke to them, saying, "All authority has been given to Me in heaven and on earth. Go therefore and make disciples of all the nations, baptizing them in the name of the Father and of the Son and of the Holy Spirit, teaching them to observe all things that I have commanded you; and lo, I am with you always, even to the end of the age." Amen. (Matthew 28:18–20 NKJV)

Paul wrote:

This is a trustworthy saying, and everyone should accept it: "Christ Jesus came into the world to save sinners"—and I am the worst of them all. But God had mercy on me so that Christ Jesus could use me as a prime example of his great patience with even the worst sinners. Then others will realize that they, too, can believe in him and receive eternal life. All honor and glory to God forever and ever! He is the eternal King, the unseen one who never dies; he alone is God. Amen. (1 Timothy 1:15–17 NLT)

But my life is worth nothing to me unless I use it for finishing the work assigned me by the Lord Jesus—the work of telling others the good news about the wonderful grace of God. (Acts 20:24 NLT)

> For *"Everyone who calls on the name of the Lord will be saved."* But how can they call on him to save them unless they believe in him? And how can they believe in him if they have never heard about him? And how can they hear about him unless someone tells them? And how will anyone go and tell them without being sent? That is why the Scriptures say, *"How beautiful are the feet of messengers who bring good news!"* (Romans 10:14–15 NLT)

The Great Commission Applies to All of Us

You can't take any of this world's material possessions with you when you leave it. So, if you are headed for an eternity in heaven, what can you take with you? People! How many people will be in heaven because you shared the good news about Jesus with them? As it stands right now, is it too many to count? Or too few? Anyone?

Do you believe in the reality of hell? Do you believe God loves you so much that He sent Jesus to die for you, and Jesus rose again? Do you believe you are going to heaven solely because of what Jesus did in paying the price for your sins? Then surely you feel the Holy Spirit's urging to tell someone else this good news.

Conversely, if you don't share this good news, do you really believe it?

After all, God's only plan for salvation is for us to tell others about Jesus. It's every Christian's job. When Jesus gave this Great Commission, He made it clear that we must tell them. Telling them is easy because God does all the work. If you're worried about your qualifications, remember, He doesn't call the equipped; He equips the called. And He calls everybody. Even me. Even you.

God used Paul, Jonah, Moses, David, and lots of other flawed, unwilling, unlikely characters in the Bible to accomplish His work. And He uses friendly but sometimes shy, mostly klutzy, and very ordinary me to share His good news. He even uses my husband, Chuck, who has a built-in discomfort with meeting people. When we simply show up, prayed up and ready to obey, God lets us watch Him work. No matter who you are, God can use you, too.

> When he (Jesus) saw the crowds, he had compassion on them because they were confused and helpless, like sheep without a shepherd. He said to his disciples, *"The harvest is great, but the workers are few. So pray to the Lord who is in charge of the harvest; ask him to send more workers into his fields."* (Matthew 9:36–38 NLT)

Will you join the harvesters?_____ Will you take someone with you to heaven? _____ One more person might go to heaven because you speak up. If it's only one, that's okay. But if you tell one person about Jesus, you'll find you just can't wait to tell the next one.

Start by committing wholeheartedly to Jesus and by accepting His Great Commission. Then let Him make you a clean and useful vessel by staying close to Him and confessing your sins as you go. Ask for the Holy Spirit's help with wisdom and obedience. Store up God's Word in your heart by reading your Bible every day, thinking about it and memorizing it, and by listening to good preachers, teachers, and speakers who constantly repeat and reinforce it. Then the Holy Spirit will bring that wealth of knowledge to mind whenever you need it.

Jesus said: *But the Helper, the Holy Spirit, whom the Father will send in My name, He will teach you all things, and bring to your remembrance all things that I said to you.* (John 14:26 NKJV)

Ask God for divine appointments. Pray for the lost or prodigal people. Pray for the Holy Spirit to open their hearts and to speak to them through you. Enlist some steadfast prayer partners. Then simply show up every day, ready to obey.

Peter wrote: *But sanctify the Lord God in your hearts, and always be ready to give a defense to everyone who asks you a reason for the hope that is in you, with meekness and fear.* (1 Peter 3:15 NKJV)

In the following passage, Paul writes that *all things are new* with you when you are in Christ. He goes on to say that God has given the *new you* the ministry of helping others to be reconciled to Him—also new in Christ.

Therefore, if anyone is in Christ, he is a new creation; old things have passed away, behold, all things have become new. Now all things are of God, who has reconciled us to Himself through Jesus Christ, and has given us the ministry of reconciliation, that is, that God was in Christ reconciling the world to Himself, not imputing their trespasses to them, and has committed to us the word of reconciliation. Now then, we are ambassadors for Christ,...(2 Corinthians 5:17–20 NKJV)

So, you see, Christians are ambassadors with an undeniable ministry, His Great Commission. However, you may think fulfilling it will take more boldness than you have. Don't worry. God does all the work through the power of His Holy Spirit. All you have to do is show up every day, prayed up and ready to obey.

Jesus said: *But you shall receive power when the Holy Spirit has come upon you; and you shall be witnesses to Me in Jerusalem, and in all Judea and Samaria, and to the end of the earth.* (Acts 1:8 NKJV)

If you don't tell someone about Jesus, you will be disobeying His Great Commission and neglecting your job as ambassador. And you will miss some sky-scraping blessings. Will you tell someone? _____

Chapter 2

If You Don't Tell Them, Who Will?

I accepted Jesus as my Savior with hundreds of others at a Billy Graham crusade. Think about it, even Billy Graham heard about Jesus from somebody. The next person who responds to the love of Jesus might share the good news with literally millions—as Billy Graham has—or he or she might even tell *your* family and friends about Jesus. For example, God led me to take my friend Stephanie to some Christian events where her walk with Jesus took a dramatic turn, which changed my life, too. Here's what happened:

Salvation Full Circle

I was raised in church in Amarillo, Texas, getting my diaper changed in the church nursery, attending children's Sunday school and vacation Bible school, squirming through "big church," stammering a line in the Christmas play, and eventually joining the church and hanging out with other teens at youth fellowship on Sunday afternoons. Even so, I had never grasped the reality that Christ died for *my* sins and that I had to receive His gift of salvation *personally*. I guess I thought I was a Christian because I went to church.

When I was about fifteen, a new minister invited the youth group to a special event at the Amarillo Arena. The arena was at the fairgrounds, and usually held the trappings of rodeos, stock shows, or country music. On this night, as I climbed the steps to the highest level, I saw a big banner: "Billy Graham Crusade." Grady Wilson and others from Billy Graham's team had come to tell me about God's simple plan: personal faith and trust in Jesus alone for salvation.

I can't remember who went along, how we got there, or exactly what Grady Wilson said. All I know is—in spite of my timidity about doing anything in front of people, and without even thinking who else was going down with me or how I might find my group and get home—when they sang, "Just as I am, I come, I come," I walked right down all those steep steps and onto the arena floor. With hundreds of others, I prayed to accept Jesus' forgiveness, and I asked Him to be my personal Lord and Savior.

After that night, slowly—because, like a dumb sheep, I sometimes wandered away from God—but surely, God started working in my life. Here's an example:

Still a teenager, I took my best friend Stephanie to a concert at my church. We heard soft folk music and a strong Christian testimony from Ed Kilbourne, Jr., a young man who obviously loved the Lord.

Later, when Stephanie and I were students at the University of Texas in Austin, I invited her to hear a speaker I had read about on a campus bulletin board. The speaker was former agnostic, Josh McDowell. The research he had conducted in an attempt to debunk Christianity had instead turned him into a passionate Christian. I had no way of knowing that, though Stephanie had accepted Jesus as her Savior when she was still in high school, lately she had been wondering whether to believe her pastor or a Mormon friend. That night Josh's answers to some tough questions locked in her faith in Jesus as the Son of God, the Way, the Truth, and the Life, without Whom no one can enter the kingdom of heaven.

Without any calculation on my part, God had worked through me to help bring Stephanie closer to Himself.

In time, Stephanie joined the Campus Crusade for Christ (now known as Cru) ministry and met an engineering student, Bob, at the meetings. They finished their degrees, got married, and committed their lives to full-time service to God. Joining the Campus Crusade staff, they even left the United States to serve in Africa and other countries. God has touched countless lives because they obeyed His call. Then one day, God's call brought them home.

***

Meanwhile, I married Chuck Middlekauff. A few years later, when Stephanie and Bob returned to the States on a furlough from Africa, they attended a ministry conference in Fort Collins, Colorado. Since the campus apartment where they were staying wasn't far from where Chuck and I were living north of Denver, they invited us over for supper.

Chuck wasn't raised in the church, didn't like it when I brought up church or God, didn't like mingling with people he hadn't met—especially missionaries—didn't care about meeting Bob and Stephanie. You're right, Chuck didn't want to go to supper at all.

"All I want to do is visit my forever friend," I begged. "And she and Bob want to meet you."

Chuck finally agreed to go. But steering the car north on Interstate 25 toward Fort Collins, he kept saying, "Don't you dare bring up anything about God!" I promised I wouldn't. Getting out of the car, he said it once more, "Don't you dare bring up anything about God!"

"I promise!" I answered.

So, I didn't bring up the subject of God. However, swallowing my first bite of Stephanie's chicken casserole, I almost choked.

Chuck had asked Bob about his job and was suddenly raising dozens of questions about God. Bob knew the Bible's answers to Chuck's questions and was patiently explaining God's creation, our sin, His love, His plan of salvation, how Jesus died on the cross to pay the penalty for our sins.

That evening Chuck accepted Christ as his Savior!

> *When His disciples heard it, they were greatly astonished, saying, "Who then can be saved?" But Jesus looked at them and said to them, "With men this is impossible, but with God all things are possible."* (Matthew 19:25–26 NKJV)

And that's what happens when God works. Try Him out. He won't disappoint you.

***

As a postscript, in the twenty-nine years of Chuck's life before that evening, no one had told him about Jesus, not even his best high school friend, a preacher's son, and not even me—he didn't want to talk with me about God. And no one has done it since.

Will you talk to someone about Jesus?_____Write down the names of five friends or relatives to invite to a concert or special event at your church. Start praying for them, asking God what part He wants you to play.

_____

_____

_____

_____

_____

Chapter 3

Quenching the Fear

If you're a Christian and you haven't taken the time to share the good news of the sacrificial love of Jesus with someone else, you're disobeying God's command, and you're missing the stacks of joy God has for you. Since you're reading this book, you must be ready to change that.

Here's the best part: you step out boldly, but you aren't alone. You have help. When you trusted Jesus as your personal Lord and Savior, you received the Holy Spirit.

> Jesus said: *But the Helper, the Holy Spirit, whom the Father will send in My name, He will teach you all things, and bring to your remembrance all things that I said to you.* (John 14:26 NKJV)

The Holy Spirit is your Helper. He doesn't make you do things. He gives you things to do, and He supplies everything you need to do them. It's simple. If you obey, you get the joy. If you don't obey, you miss the joy. As Henry Blackaby says in his book, *Experiencing God*, it's a matter of finding out where God is working and joining Him there. God does all the work, and you just show up, prayed up and available to do whatever the Holy Spirit gives you to do.

> Jesus said: *But you shall receive power when the Holy Spirit has come upon you; and you shall be witnesses to Me in Jerusalem, and in all Judea and Samaria, and to the end of the earth.* (Acts 1:8 NKJV)

So, God has given all of us the ways and means: His Own power through the Holy Spirit.

However, even knowing that you have this tremendous power, when it comes to sharing the good news about Jesus, you may feel the same way I felt the very first time I tried: I was willing, but I was chicken.

I had the same basic problem that causes many people to be afraid of public speaking: not having any idea what to say. Pastors who talked about the subject of personal evangelism simply exhorted the church. They challenged us to do it, but they didn't explain how to do it or offer any role-play practice. They said they had brought up the subject of Jesus with folks on airplanes, etc., but they never filled in the details of those conversations. So, let's face it, I was clueless, frozen-in-my-tracks-scared—worse than I felt in that Christmas play when I was little. Maybe you feel the same way. We're not alone. Paul wrote to the believers in Corinth:

> *I came to you in weakness—timid and trembling.* (1 Corinthians 2:3 NLT)

But that didn't stop him, did it?

Maybe you can identify with some of my pathetic experiences.

The Ladies in the Lunchroom

Once in the mid 1970s, I had a perfect opportunity to speak up for Jesus at work. Five women were sitting around the table in the lunchroom. "I think everyone is going to heaven in their own way," Colleen said. The others all nodded.

I knew what she said wasn't true. But I sat there like a doorknob. It wasn't that I was ashamed of Jesus. And it certainly wasn't that I wanted the women in the lunchroom to miss out on a relationship—an eternity—with God. I just had no idea how to tell them about my Savior. And I didn't want to get anyone mad at me.

> But Jesus said: *And do not fear those who kill the body but cannot kill the soul. But rather fear Him who is able to destroy both soul and body in hell.* (Matthew 10:28 NKJV)

List some times when you knew someone was wrong in what they said about the way to get to heaven, but you chickened out.

_____

_____

_____

My Daddy Knew Jesus

After that pitiful day in the lunchroom, a few years passed. Then my wonderful daddy died. He was just fifty-six. Cancer had been battering his body, so it wasn't a total shock. But I was going to miss him.

I was working nights at the post office in Denver, and before I could take time off to attend his funeral, I had to work one more shift. So, I went to work. I was sad, but I had a smile on my face and bounce in my step because I knew my daddy had a personal relationship with Jesus and was with Him. When others at work heard about my loss, they asked me, "How can you still be smiling?" I simply said, "Because I know Jesus. And so did my daddy." I'm sure God used this small testimony to add someone to His kingdom. But I didn't get to celebrate with them because I didn't know how to tell them more about my Savior.

More years went by. I sat back on the laurels of having played a small part in my missionary friend Stephanie's start in ministry. But I wasn't bearing any fruit. I wasn't glorifying the Father.

> Jesus said: _By this My Father is glorified, that you bear much fruit._ (John 15:8 NKJV)

Are you still resting on somebody else's laurels? _____

The Guest Speaker

Eventually, things changed. Chuck and I found a good Bible-based church, LIFE Fellowship, in a suburb north of Denver. One Sunday, our pastor, Ed Bulkley, ended his sermon by saying, "Bring a pocket-sized Bible with you to church next Sunday. I have invited a guest speaker who is going to teach you how to share your faith."

The next day, Chuck and I went to the bookstore after work and bought our little Bibles. When Sunday came, Bibles in hand, we sat at the front of the worship center. Pastor Ed introduced evangelist Bill Fay, saying, "He's going to show us how to share our faith without an argument." That was exactly what I needed. Maybe you need it, too. Here's how it went:

First, Bill touched upon the dreadful details of his earlier life. With ties to the mob and prostitution, gambling and racketeering, he was basically corrupt. But that was before he gave his life to Jesus. After Jesus took over Bill's life, the brand new man wanted to tell everyone the good news. As Bill worked furiously to do so, the Holy Spirit revealed to him that it wasn't about what Bill did, but about what God did.

"God's Word does the work," Bill said. "And you'll be surprised how often conversations naturally lead toward God. Even someone's swearing can lead to a conversation about God—without an argument."

In our front-row seats, Chuck and I leaned forward. This was getting good.

Bill gave us some questions to ask when a conversation turns toward God. His point was that you don't argue. You're asking these questions to find out about their spiritual beliefs, and no matter what they say, they can't give wrong answers because they're telling *their* beliefs. You don't have to dispute anything. However, if they don't say that the only reason God would let them into heaven is that they have put their faith and trust in Jesus alone, or if they say they think they're going to hell, you ask another question: "Would it be okay if I share what the Bible says?" If they say "Yes," you have permission to share the scriptures.

I was having my own thoughts, *What if the person gets mad at me for bringing up the subject of God at all?*

Bill was ahead of me, saying, "If they don't want to talk about God at that moment, simply change the subject. Start praying for them silently and include them in your daily prayers."

That's perfect, I thought. *But there's no way I'm going to remember all those questions.*

"Did everyone bring a small Bible?" Bill was asking. "You're going to write the questions in the front of your Bible." He repeated the questions as we wrote them down.

"Again, if the person wants to know what the Bible says," he continued, "you have permission to show them God's Word. And the scriptures speak for themselves."

Then Bill gave us a set of scriptures. He told us to put a marker at the first one. Then he waited while we found and marked each scripture then wrote the address for the next scripture at the top of the page. "That way," he said, "you can find them easily, without distracting from God's work." He reemphasized that God's Word does the convicting through the Holy Spirit. So you don't have much to say.

Then he had us write down five more questions that would help us find out whether or not the person understands the significance of the gift God has given us in Christ Jesus. The final question—the most important question in anyone's life—is, "Are you ready to invite Jesus into your life?"

"Be patient," he added. "When you ask these questions, don't open your mouth. Wait for your lost friend to break the silence. Let the Holy Spirit work."

> Jesus said: *Most assuredly, I say to you, he who hears My word and believes in Him who sent Me has everlasting life, and shall not come into judgment, but has passed from death into life.* (John 5:24 NKJV)

It all starts with realizing that the gospel applies to you personally. The decision to trust Christ alone for your salvation is yours alone. Anyone can begin the relationship to God with a simple prayer, something like this:

My God and Heavenly Father, I'm a sinner, and I know I deserve hell. I'm sorry I sinned against you. Please forgive me. I repent (turn away) from my sins. I believe Jesus died to pay the penalty for all my sins, and rose from the grave. I trust Jesus alone, and not my works, for my salvation, and make Him Lord of my life. Thank you God for the forgiveness and everlasting life I now have through Jesus. Since I will need a lot of help to have the relationship You desire with me, please empower me with Your Holy Spirit, and make me the person You want me to be. Amen.

If you are genuinely committing your life to Jesus, with the belief that He alone paid for your sins and rose again, you are born again and you are a brand new baby Christian, a new creation!

> *Therefore, if anyone is in Christ, he is a new creation, old things have passed away; behold, all things have become new.* (2 Corinthians 5:17 NKJV)

If you are leading someone in this prayer, pause after each few words for him or her to pray after you. Whether it's you or someone else making this decision, a celebration begins in heaven.

However, if the answer to the last question is "No," ask the person "Why?" and again wait patiently, silently, and prayerfully for the answer. For each ensuing answer, continue to ask why. Often the person's answers to "Why?" will bring such conviction that the answer changes to "Yes." But if the conversation just ends, change the subject and leave it to God.

***

Armed with our marked-up Bibles and this simple approach—theoretically speaking—Chuck and I were ready to tell people about Jesus without an argument. But even though God was drawing us to share our faith with others, we were still shaking in our shoes.

It didn't matter. God was already busy making appointments for us.

***

Since Bill Fay taught us how to share our faith without an argument, he has written the book, ***Share Jesus without Fear,*** published by LifeWay's B&H Publishing Group. Besides listing the questions and scriptures, his book is full of answers to those difficult questions, doubts, uncertainties, and excuses people often give as they encounter Jesus through you. Another good resource is ***The Case for Faith*** by Lee Strobel. (See the Resources and Contact Information at the end of the book for details.)

Ideas from ***Share Jesus without Fear*** by William Fay, © Copyright 1999 B&H Publishing Group, used by permission.

***

Paul wrote: *It is God who enables us, along with you, to stand firm for Christ. He has commissioned us, and he has identified us as his own by placing the Holy Spirit in our hearts as the first installment that guarantees everything he has promised us.* (2 Corinthians 1:21–22 NLT)

If this simple approach appeals to you, purchase a small Bible and mark it up, using the questions and scriptures in Bill Fay's book or other gospel scriptures.

When will you start? Today's date_____

Shaking in My Shoes

After evangelist Bill Fay taught the congregation how to share our faith that Sunday, Pastor Ed walked back onto the stage and challenged us quaking pew sitters to tell just one person about Jesus during the next week. "Write down a name!" he boomed in his loudest preacher voice.

I still have the piece of paper where I wrote, "Tell Sharon about Jesus (ask) by Friday." We left the worship center, convicted, equipped, and challenged. Here's what happened:

I handled the commercial accounts at a small insurance agency. Jane (late twenties and soft blonde curls) was the receptionist. She answered the phone like a robot, no friendliness in her voice at all. Jerry (past retirement age) was the boss. He came into the office at around ten every morning—and read the newspaper. He occasionally called before he came to work, to see if Jane sounded like she was smiling. She didn't.

For my first day on the job, Jerry had been in the office early. Meeting me at the door when I arrived at eight that Monday morning, he walked me to his office, sat down behind his desk, and motioned me to a chair across from him. Beginning to tell me about the agency and its accounts, he seemed nervous, distracted. Finally, he got around to sharing his problem. Besides the commercial lines service representative I was replacing, his sales guy and the personal lines person had quit over the weekend. Everybody but Jane. And me.

So, even though Jane knew nothing about insurance, and she was not the greatest receptionist, Jerry needed her. And Jerry really needed me. For a few weeks, I handled all the commercial lines stuff. For the personal lines accounts, I took care of claims and urgent matters and stacked the other requests and files on the vacant personal lines desk. Jane answered the phone. And Jerry read the newspaper. With all that work to do, I didn't have time to get to know Jane.

After a few weeks of this craziness, Jerry hired Sharon. She looked like a high school kid, but I immediately sensed that she was extremely bright—a redheaded, take-charge dynamo. Though she later told me the stacks of files on her desk had overwhelmed her that first day, Sharon had plowed right in, handling all the personal accounts.

As the months rolled by, my first impressions were confirmed: Sharon was terrific. That's why I had written her name down when Pastor Ed challenged us to tell someone about Jesus that week. I have to admit, however, that even though Sharon was twenty years younger than I was (she told me she was twenty-three), and I liked and respected her a lot, she intimidated me.

But taking Pastor Ed's witnessing assignment seriously, I went to work each day that week, determined to tell Sharon about Jesus, well, at least to ask her Bill Fay's questions. However, by lunchtime on Friday, I still couldn't bring myself to begin that conversation. The Holy Spirit was convicting me: *"You still haven't shared My love with anyone."*

I was trying to gather up the nerve to ask Sharon the questions during lunch when Jane appeared at my desk, her face all puffy and red and tears streaming down her cheeks.

Obviously, Jane was not Sharon, but there she was, standing by my desk.

"Please help me!" she sobbed.

Jane might have been the one who was crying, but as I grabbed the little marked-up Bible out of my purse, I was shaking.

"Could you catch the phones?" I said over my shoulder to Sharon as I led Jane into the small conference room in a corner of the office. I closed the door, and we sat down at the glass table.

"I'm in trouble with alcohol," she managed to say between sobs.

There was no way I could talk Jane through her alcohol problem. I knew a lot about commercial insurance, but this was totally out of my league.

"It must be deeper than that," I said, fumbling for something to say.

Then the Holy Spirit took over.

Opening my Bible and reading right off of the front flyleaf, I began to ask Bill Fay's questions, ending with, "Where would you go if you died today?"

To each question, Jane whimpered, "I don't know."

Well, at least we knew where she stood. And maybe that was the first time she had thought about it.

"Do you mind if I share some Bible verses with you?" I asked.

"Okay," she said, starting to calm down a little.

My hands rattled the thin pages of my little Bible as I scrambled to find the first scripture. *This seemed so much easier when Bill Fay did it,* I said to myself.

I eventually found it. Slowly but surely I turned to the references I had written upside down on the tops of the pages, and we went through all the verses. When we finished, I looked up at Jane. "So, are you a sinner? Would you like forgiveness for your sins? Would you like to invite Jesus into your life?" I asked, managing to wait silently after each question.

Though she answered "Yes" to the first two questions, she said "No" to the last. When I asked her why, she said, "I'm not ready yet. I still have too many questions about all of that."

We had used up most of our lunch hour, so it didn't seem like the time and place for me to try to answer her questions. I asked if I could pray for her, and she nodded.

"Heavenly Father, please give Jane Your healing and peace," I prayed, "and open her heart to Your Word. Amen."

She blew her nose on a crumpled tissue, looked up at me, and even smiled a little.

"Can we get together somewhere after work?" I asked. She suggested a park she knew about. "You've met my husband, Chuck," I said. "He's picking me up at five. Would it would be okay if he comes, too?" She nodded again, and we walked back to our desks.

That evening, sitting at a picnic table in the park, as best we could, Chuck and I answered Jane's questions about God. We told her that He created the universe, flowers, birds, and butterflies, and that He loves her. That we have all sinned, but He loves her enough to send His only Son, Jesus, to die in her place for her sins.

But she was still not ready to commit her life to Jesus.

Not long after that, Jerry finally fired Jane. Even after she found another job, Chuck and I saw her a few times. She told us she always knew she wasn't cut out to be a receptionist, but she was enjoying her new job in advertising production. She was thinking about what we had told her about God, but she still wasn't ready to commit.

Since then, we've lost touch with Jane.

However, Chuck and I had gotten over the petrifying fear of sharing our faith the first time. We had discovered that it wasn't life threatening. And God had already changed us.

It wasn't that same week, but I finally did talk to Sharon. Summoning all the newfound courage I could muster, I asked her, "Do you have any spiritual beliefs?"

"That is a private matter," she said sharply. "And I don't want to discuss it at work."

"What about some other time?" I asked.

"No," she said with finality.

Well, that wasn't how I wanted the conversation with Sharon to go, but I found out it wasn't life threatening either. We still got along afterwards.

Beginning with Jane and Sharon, I've found that the more times I honor God by following His lead, the easier it gets. Even though I don't know what happened with Jane and Sharon after that, I know I planted seeds of faith in their lives, and it's God's job to make them ready for harvest.

***

Bill Fay's training in how to use the Bible—and our pastor's challenge to tell someone that week—turned out to be the best things God could have done to give me the nerve to start sharing my faith. When God opened the door for that divine appointment with Jane, I knew what to do, so I didn't chicken out.

But I'm still a regular person. I must admit that I can think back on dozens of times when God has opened doors and I didn't follow Him in. And I know there were hundreds more when I didn't even notice a door. However, when I've followed the Holy Spirit's guidance, I've had the pure joy of being right in God's presence when someone is born into His kingdom—literally hundreds of times.

It all started after I made the commitment to obey the Holy Spirit. It happened when I obeyed Him, even when I was shaking in my shoes. And, though I feel awful for a while when someone says "No" or "NO!" I never regret obeying God's lead. I pray for those people and go on. And He shows His loving touch by supplying a strong encourager in my life—usually immediately.

The Holy Spirit will help you, too. The courage comes from caring about others' eternal lives and from believing what you know and knowing what you believe. The late Adrian Rogers, a much-admired Bible preacher, used to tell a story about a chaplain who came up to talk with him after a sermon. The chaplain said he had been an atheist until he happened to tune in a radio to one of Rogers' messages. When Rogers asked why he listened to the whole message that led him to turn his life over to Jesus, the chaplain said that it wasn't because he believed in the Bible—or even in God—at the time, but because he believed Adrian Rogers believed.

> Jesus said: *But when the Helper comes, whom I shall send to you from the Father, the Spirit of truth who proceeds from the Father, He will testify of Me. And you also will bear witness,...*(John 15:26–27 NKJV)

Write down the name of someone you will introduce to Jesus this week.

_____

A David Story

After my job at the insurance agency eventually fizzled, I took temporary jobs for a while. As short-term data entry employees at a computer technology company in Boulder, Colorado, David and I shared an office in the center of the building. Tapping away on computer keyboards, we entered information about the company's customers, one record after another. Beyond the occasional comment about someone whose name was Donald Duck or other trivial matters, the windowless space generally held only the sounds of clicking keys and shuffling papers. When lunchtime came around, we usually left our little room to find some daylight and breathe some Rocky Mountain air.

David, slender, clean-cut, and in his early twenties—about half my age—seemed like a nice enough guy, but we were pretty much strangers. One day it was threatening rain, as dreary outside as it was inside, so we both sat at our desks during lunch. Somehow, we broke the ice, and David started telling me about his dreams of becoming a computer programmer.

"How would you do that?" I asked.

"Well, I guess I would have to go back to school," David answered. Then he started thinking out loud about what kind of school he might attend.

"You're going to be that school's best student," I said. He laughed.

A month or so later, David arrived in our office with books under his arm. "I signed up for school," he announced. "My first class is after work today."

During our breaks over the next weeks, David shared his new adventure with me. It seems that programming classes begin with a big dose of math and bigger doses of computer logic and other techie stuff. Most of what he said about it went right over my head and hit the wall behind me. But I enjoyed his enthusiasm.

A few months later, during another lunchtime discussion, David told me he had accepted my challenge to be the best student. He was doing double the assigned work. If the instructor gave the class the odd-numbered practice problems, David did all the even ones, too. He was making straight A's.

"I'm so proud of you," I said.

I heard a small voice (not David's) say, *"Ask him about his spiritual beliefs. The door's open."*

Only the Holy Spirit would speak to me like that. I felt uncomfortable getting out my little marked-up Bible at work, but I sort of remembered the questions.

"You are going to be the best student!" I said. "But I'm curious about your spiritual standing. Do you have any spiritual beliefs?"

I had blurted out that last bit in a rush. I take what Christ did for me very seriously, so I had to say something. Before I had committed any scriptures (besides John 3:16) to memory, and before I had a tract to use, God was compelling me to share His good news with others, and He had set up the opportunity with David.

"Sure," he said, and he started describing a faith I had never heard of, finishing with a flourish, "The afterlife will be a series of reincarnations, sort of like the spokes on a wheel."

"Where did you learn all of this?" I asked.

"I made it up myself," he said, and went on to tell me a little more about his system, which seemed to be a jumble of New Age and other religions where a person could work his own way to God.

When he finished, I asked, "Would you mind if I share my beliefs?"

We had time left on our lunch hour, and he said he didn't mind. So I explained as best I could that I believe the Bible is the true and reliable source of God's story, that it tells us God created us, that we have all sinned and fallen short of our holy God's requirements, but God loves us so much that He sent His only Son Jesus to pay in full for our sins by dying on the cross, and that Jesus rose again. I have to say that I needed help from the Holy Spirit to say that smoothly and clearly. But with His help, anyone can say that much, even without a marked up Bible.

David fastened his eyes on me and listened. Then the conversation ended. "I appreciate your sharing this with me," he said. "But I'm not interested in discussing the subject again."

God was working in me and in David that day, opening the door for the conversation, giving me the courage to step through it, and magnetizing his full attention. I may not know the outcome until I get to heaven, but I had planted the seed God gave me. Only God can finish the work.

Since then I have been praying for God to open David's heart and eyes. And I have been praising God because the experience made it easier for me to share the good news about Jesus again. After all, I didn't die right there on the spot when David rejected God's promises, and David and I were still friends afterwards.

Try it yourself. Ask someone about his or her spiritual beliefs and let them tell you. If the Holy Spirit opens the door, explain the good news. If the person rejects the message, remember they're not rejecting you. They're rejecting Jesus. Pray for them and move on, leaving it for Him to complete the work. Here's what Jesus said:

> *And whoever will not receive you nor hear your words, when you depart from that house or city, shake off the dust from your feet.* (Matthew 10:14 NKJV)

Write down the names of several people from your office or neighborhood. Pray for them, and be ready for opportunities to share the gospel with them.

_____

_____

What Happened with Dennis?

My husband, Chuck Middlekauff, is a full-time fine artist. One of the first galleries to show his work crowned the top of a pass near Allenspark, Colorado. At this stage in its life, this one-hundred-year-old building held Chuck's bold cowboy paintings on its rustic log walls, along with assorted pottery and drawings and paintings of mountainous landscapes, colorful flowers, and indigenous critters, all by several other local artists.

Dennis Reinke was one of the other artists. Each time we delivered Chuck's paintings or visited the gallery to see how sales were going, we were drawn to Dennis' stunning watercolor interpretations of Colorado sights. Because artists rarely show up at the same time to drop their work off at galleries, we usually don't meet the other artists. We had never actually seen Dennis. But we felt like we knew him because we were so attached to his work.

We finally met Dennis when the gallery held a show for all of its artists. As art shows often go, about the only lookers who came that Saturday afternoon were the artists. And the artists weren't buying anything. So, we sat on the gray planks of the gallery's front porch, soaking up the sunshine, breathing dry, pine-scented mountain air, and talking about art.

Besides the fact that we felt like we knew him through his artwork, Dennis was a likeable guy, and he was about our age. We ended up talking to him more than the other artists. He had been an architect and had even spent some time as a bricklayer. No wonder his miniature studies of Colorado subjects reflected that sort of detail, precision, and craftsmanship.

As the shadows of the lodgepole pine trees stretched across Highway 7 in front of the gallery, we got in our cars to head home. "I've fixed up that old red barn in Allenspark as a studio." Dennis said through his car window. "Stop by and see me if you're in the neighborhood." We nodded and waved.

"We're never doing another show at that gallery," Chuck muttered as we drove back down the mountain to our apartment in Longmont (about thirty miles north of Denver and maybe twenty-five miles southeast of Allenspark). "But I do hope we'll stay in touch with Dennis." This last part was a rare statement from Chuck, who usually didn't want to clutter his life with too many relationships.

The next time we dropped by the gallery, we asked the owner if he knew where Dennis lived.

"He rented an old red barn across the highway," he offered. "But I don't know exactly where it is."

"Well, Allenspark isn't much of a town," I said. "How hard can it be to find a red barn?"

Chuck and I drove the dirt roads of the mountain town until we found a big, red building. It wasn't really a barn, but it was the only red building. It had to be Dennis' place, so we took a chance and knocked on the door. Though he wasn't expecting us, Dennis invited us right in and took us on a grand tour of the place. Besides ample living quarters, he had lots of extra space for his art studio and talked about his plans for fixing up the old building.

Then, a few months later, the gallery owner told us Dennis had lost a close family member, was deeply depressed, and hadn't painted anything since his loss.

Hoping to cheer him up a little, we stopped by the red barn. His car was out front, so we tapped on the door several times. Dennis eventually answered and invited us in, but unlike our last visit, he was simply listless.

"I'm broke," he said. "The owner is fixing to throw me out, and I have no idea what I'm going to do."

We didn't have any money to give him, but we had gas in our car. "Let's take a drive," Chuck invited. "You need to get the kinks out." Dennis agreed to go.

As Chuck steered the car through the mountains, he somehow steered the conversation to the subject of God. Then he asked Dennis, "How about you? Do you have any spiritual beliefs?" Dennis had little to say, but he wasn't avoiding the subject.

We didn't have the Bible verses memorized, and it seemed too awkward to read the scriptures over the seatbacks. But we explained to Dennis how much God loved him, that He had good plans for him, that Jesus died to pay for his sins, and that He rose again. We explained that trusting Jesus is the only way to start a relationship with God.

"My brother has been telling me the same thing," he said. "I'm just not ready to commit."

We asked if we could pray for him, for his healing, for his comfort and peace. He didn't mind if we did, so we pulled over in a wide spot on the highway, grabbed his hands, and prayed right there in the car. By the time we dropped him off at the red barn, Dennis had brightened visibly.

We moved away from Colorado for several years, and the next time we drove by the red barn, boards covered the windows and the porch sagged in the middle. Dennis was gone.

Then one evening several years later, the phone rang. It was Dennis. "I have the best news I could ever give you!" he said. "I've committed my life to Jesus as my Lord and Savior! I knew you would want to know."

***

As I was writing this story about Dennis, I Googled his name on the Internet. Sure enough, his artwork was there, bigger, bolder, brighter, and still just as rich in detail. His email address was there, too, so we sent him a message. He emailed us back to let us know that—almost twenty years later—he's still on track with his Lord.

> *Jesus said to her* [Martha, Lazarus' sister], *"I am the resurrection and the life. He who believes in Me, though he may die, he shall live."* (John 11:25 NKJV)

Are you on track with Him? Who in your life needs new hope that can only be found in Jesus? Write down some names, so the very next time you get together, you will be ready to ask questions that will lead them to—or back to—God.

_____

_____

_____

_____

Chapter 4

Taking F.A.I.T.H. to the Streets

I grew up in Amarillo, Texas, and at age nineteen, I moved to Austin to attend the University of Texas. A few months after I graduated, I met Chuck Middlekauff. We fell right in love and got married in a matter of six months. Shortly after that, we packed all of our stuff in a Pontiac Tempest and moved to Colorado, where we lived for twenty years; then we called Southern California home for five years. After all those years away, Chuck and I returned to Austin, ready to help care for our aging parents. We had gotten away from regular church attendance for several years, but we had studied the Bible, listened to Bible-based radio and TV preachers, and prayed. God had taken us to a place in our lives where we were ready for a serious spiritual growth spurt. It happened like this:

On Sunday mornings, we watched televised services from Austin's Great Hills Baptist Church, where Preacher Harold O'Chester taught straight from the Bible. In early 2003, Chuck decided we should start attending Great Hills, even though we hadn't been Baptists, and Preacher was threatening to retire. After all, we really didn't think he would leave. But on the first Sunday we visited, Preacher surrendered the church to thirty-five-year-old Michael Lewis from Savannah, Georgia.

The next few months revealed our new pastor's passion for sharing the good news about Christ. One member, Steve, told us he had flown Pastor Lewis over Austin in his small plane. Looking down on the city, our new pastor had wept and prayed over "all the lost people under those housetops."

One of the first Great Hills members we met was Maxine. We had barely exchanged names and comments about how much we admired the new pastor when she practically demanded, "You have to take the 'Experiencing God' class I just heard about. It starts next Sunday."

In spite of the fact that we don't like a person we don't even know telling us what we "have" to do (spiritually or otherwise) and the fact that Chuck usually resists group situations, we found ourselves in the "Experiencing God" class at five o'clock the next Sunday afternoon.

During the eight-week course, Scott, Brent, Chuck and I, and class leader David watched and discussed Henry Blackaby's video presentations and study guide. All five of us took great leaps in our individual walks of faith as we learned that God is always working and He extends an open invitation for us to join Him in His work.

Blackaby pointed out that the people God chose to do His big jobs in the Bible had moments of serious doubts about their own abilities to do those jobs. Blackaby called each of those moments "a crisis of faith." However, after varying amounts of resistance, the obedient Bible heroes eventually discovered that when they just showed up—prayed up and ready to submit to God's leadership—God did His awesome work, in them and through them.

It's still true for us, and for you. As Blackaby told us, it's a matter of finding out where God is working and joining Him there.

Not long after the "Experiencing God" class ended, Chuck and I went even farther outside our comfort zones and joined our pastor and hundreds of others, knocking on doors all across Austin, telling whoever answered those doors about Jesus, and inviting them to Sunday school.

The door-knocking adventures started simply enough. One Sunday morning, Pastor Lewis invited the two thousand worshipers to a "Sunday School Banquet" that same evening. He didn't give any details about what was to take place, and I sometimes wonder what he expected.

However, Chuck and I were curious enough to show up at church that night. We found the Atrium, a big multi-purpose room, stuffed with more than seven hundred people. Eating barbeque, potato salad, and beans, they overflowed the main floor and filled rows of tables the janitors grabbed out of

Sunday school classrooms and set up along a mezzanine level above. I didn't think about it at the time, but stretching that barbeque to feed all those people must have been one of those loaves and fishes miracles.

Bobby Welch, who with Johnny Hunt and others had co-created F.A.I.T.H. Sunday School Evangelism, was our speaker. He explained that we were going to learn how to share the gospel using the F.A.I.T.H. outline. Then we were going to teach others to do it, just as Paul wrote to Timothy:

> *You therefore, my son, be strong in the grace that is in Christ Jesus. And the things that you have heard from me among many witnesses, commit these to faithful men who will be able to teach others also.* (2 Timothy 2:1–2 NKJV)

Mr. Welch offered powerful reasons to share our faith, and he defused a bunch of excuses. That was all good, but what really grabbed our attention was a man who stepped up to the microphone and told us his story. He had been in the hospital a year earlier when his daughter shared this same F.A.I.T.H. outline and introduced him to Christ. After he trusted Christ as his own savior, he was so grateful for God's forgiveness and the assurance of his place in heaven that he simply had to tell others. In the ensuing year, God had worked through and in him for the new births of at least two hundred more baby Christians.

We wanted to do that, too. After signing commitment cards, we prayed with Pastor Lewis that God would use us mightily.

On Monday night a week later, we joined five hundred of the seven hundred, who had eaten barbecue at the Sunday School Banquet and were back in the Atrium, ready to work.

"Over the next fifteen-week 'semester,'" Pastor Lewis told us, "I'm going to teach you how to make F.A.I.T.H. visits." Then he added, "And you are going to learn some scriptures."

Yeah, right, I said to myself. I was willing to try to learn the F.A.I.T.H. outline and scriptures in fifteen weeks. But I was not at all sure my brain, which leaked out names, numbers, and lots of other information I tried to store in it, was up to the task. It was one of those times our "Experiencing God" video teacher, Henry Blackaby, had called a "crisis of faith."

But it wasn't up to me. It was up to God.

It started with prayer. One of the most important ingredients of F.A.I.T.H. was that each team member was to sign up at least two prayer partners, who would pray for that person throughout the semester. The team member was to give ongoing reports about what God was doing. I enlisted Pam, a Christian friend from work and a true prayer warrior (who has continued to pray for me since 2003). And I signed up church friends Raymond (who has cerebral palsy, and can't go out on visits, but is the best prayer partner and cheerleader anyone could have) and Nancy (a Sunday school classmate who has muscular dystrophy and is also a tremendous prayer warrior). Chuck recruited Dick and his wife Ann (a married couple, who at ninety-two and eighty-five were dedicated Christian soldiers). They were faithful to remind each other—compounding the prayer covering. And they held Chuck strictly accountable for those weekly reports.

For fifteen straight Mondays, the divinely assigned teams of three sat at tables in the Atrium. One team member was our "leader." The other two were "learners." The first leaders were the church staff and deacons, the Sunday school directors and teachers (who had learned F.A.I.T.H. in a weeklong crash course) and Pastor Lewis.

Each Monday, after our "team time" of praying together and practicing our scriptures, Pastor Lewis taught us how to make F.A.I.T.H. visits, using his experiences, F.A.I.T.H. videos, and a workbook. His enthusiasm for sharing the love of Jesus and the gospel message spread through the group like a grassfire on a hot windy day.

Meanwhile, between Monday F.A.I.T.H. nights, we prayed and we learned the outline and scriptures. One section at a time, one scripture after another, Chuck and I practiced the transitions and verses aloud when he drove me to and from work, and I said them to myself when I was alone for the drive— until we had committed the whole thing to memory.

As I said, it was extremely unlikely that I could ever learn all those scriptures in my own strength. But I did, with God's help. With God's help, you can do it, too. Using the F.A.I.T.H. outline that follows, take one transition at a time and one scripture at a time, and add another transition and another scripture—until you have it.

We continued to meet for one fifteen-week semester, and then another, and another, for increasing levels of training and discipleship. Ignoring our fears, the randomly but prayerfully assigned teams headed out into the Austin neighborhoods to knock on strange doors and tell strangers the good news. Hundreds of those strangers and neighbors found new life in Christ because the F.A.I.T.H. teams showed up ready to work each week. And God, as He promises in His Word, worked though us.

We got to talk about Jesus on someone's porch, and we sometimes had the joy of being right there when someone invited Jesus into a life. One of my other favorite parts of F.A.I.T.H. Sunday School Evangelism training was returning to the church after our Monday night visits and hearing the other teams' triumphant tales. Our theme verse was:

> *Those who sow in tears shall reap in joy. He who continually goes forth weeping, bearing seed for sowing, shall doubtless come again with rejoicing, bringing his sheaves with him.* (Psalm 126:5 NKJV)

The following stories tell about a few of those encounters. They happened because we took the time to work with God to learn the scriptures, because we committed a bunch of Monday nights to learn how to share our faith, and because we trusted God to work through us as we shared His good news.

> *Instead, you must worship Christ as Lord of your life. And if someone asks about your Christian hope, always be ready to explain it. But do this in a gentle and respectful way.* (1 Peter 3:15 NLT)

Because your testimony about what Jesus has done in your life will powerfully demonstrate God's love, you don't have to memorize the scriptures to introduce someone to Him. But taking the time to learn the F.A.I.T.H. outline, which appears on the next pages, prepares you to share the Biblical reasons for your faith in any circumstances. You can even use the time when you are stuck at stoplights to memorize and rehearse the outline and verses. Write down some other times you can practice. And start today.

_____

_____

_____

_____

F.A.I.T.H. Outline

Key Question: In your personal opinion, what do you understand it takes for a person to go to heaven?

Transition Statement: I'd like to share with you how the Bible answers this question, if it is all right. There is a word that can be used to answer this question: F.A.I.T.H. (spell out on fingers).

F is for FORGIVENESS.

We cannot have eternal life and heaven without God's forgiveness.

"In Him [meaning Jesus] we have redemption through His blood, the forgiveness of sins."—Ephesians 1:7a, NKJV

A is for AVAILABLE.

Forgiveness is available. It is—

- AVAILABLE FOR ALL

"For God so loved the world that He gave His only begotten Son, that whoever believes in Him should not perish but have everlasting life."—John 3:16, NKJV

- BUT NOT AUTOMATIC

"Not everyone who says to Me, 'Lord, Lord,' shall enter the kingdom of heaven."—Matthew 7:21a, NKJV

I is for IMPOSSIBLE.

It is impossible for God to allow sin into heaven.

GOD IS

- LOVE

John 3:16, NKJV

- JUST

"For judgment is without mercy."—James 2:13a, NKJV

MAN IS

- SINFUL

"For all have sinned and fall short of the glory of God."—Romans 3:23, NKJV

Question: But how can a sinful person enter heaven, where God allows no sin?

T is for TURN.

Question: If you were driving down the road and someone asked you to turn, what would he or she be asking you to do? *(change direction)*

Turn means repent.

- TURN from something—sin and self.

"But unless you repent you will all likewise perish."—Luke 13:3b, NKJV

- TURN to Someone—trust Christ only.

(The Bible tells us that) *"Christ died for our sins according to the Scriptures; and that He was buried, and that He rose again the third day according to the Scriptures."*—1 Corinthians 15:3b–4, NKJV

"If you confess with your mouth the Lord Jesus and believe in your heart that God has raised Him from the dead, you will be saved."—Romans 10:9, NKJV

H is for HEAVEN.

Heaven is eternal life.

- HERE

"I have come that they may have life, and that they may have it more abundantly."—John 10:10b, NKJV

- HEREAFTER

"And if I go and prepare a place for you, I will come again and receive you to Myself; that where I am, there you may be also."—John 14:3, NKJV

- HOW

How can a person have God's forgiveness, heaven and eternal life, and Jesus as personal Savior and Lord?

Inquire: Understanding what we have shared, would you like to receive this forgiveness by trusting Christ as your personal Savior and Lord?

F.A.I.T.H.—Forsaking All I Trust Him

The Jewish Neighbor

The very first Monday night of F.A.I.T.H. was orientation. We and five hundred other recruits who showed up to learn how to share our faith were relieved when Pastor Lewis told us we didn't have to ring anyone's doorbell that night. Seeing on assignment sheets that Chuck and I were on different teams, we took seats beside our new team members and waited to hear what our pastor meant by "F.A.I.T.H. Sunday School Evangelism."

You can see that the F.A.I.T.H. outline on the preceding pages starts with a question: "In your personal opinion, what do you understand that it takes for a person to go to heaven?" The rest consists of transitions and scriptures that explain God's good news, using the five letters in F.A.I.T.H.

Pastor Lewis showed us a DVD of a F.A.I.T.H. team visit, in which the learners conquered their fears of knocking on that first front door, and the leader went through F.A.I.T.H. with the man who answered. The guy in the video did it so smoothly and naturally, we were sure we could do it, too.

Pastor explained to us that he had asked all of the Sunday school teachers and directors, his staff members, and the deacons to do a weeklong crash course in F.A.I.T.H. Each one was to learn the outline and scriptures and prepare to act as "leader" for two "learners." Those of us who were learners would have fifteen weeks to learn it, but our team leaders had done the crash course only a few weeks before. We could only hope they had it down.

The next Monday, five hundred people showed up again, ready to go into the neighborhoods of Austin. The two learners on each team practiced the first lines of the F.A.I.T.H. outline with their leader. Then Pastor Lewis led a thirty-minute training session, giving more details about how we would visit homes in our teams of three: two men and a woman, or two women and a man. Our mission was to share the good news about Christ, and to start the discipleship process by inviting people to our Sunday school class. Pastor finished by praying for our safe travels and for the people in the houses we would visit.

All the F.A.I.T.H. teams swarmed from the church to the parking lot and climbed into cars, SUV's, and pickup trucks. I had never met the two men on my team. Bob was our leader, and Richard was the other learner. After we settled in the car, Richard prayed for our team again, and, as designated driver for the evening, I started the car. We were about to experience God's precise timing.

Opening our team's three-ring binder, Bob found pages describing three possible visits. The top page described Kathy, a woman about our age who had visited our church a few times.

"Let's go see her," Bob said. "Surely she'll be friendly. We can invite her to another worship service and Sunday school."

We all agreed. With Bob reading directions from the computer-generated page in the binder, I drove northwest on a nearby freeway for more than twenty minutes, eventually coming to the Austin outskirts town of Leander. Struggling to follow the increasingly complex directions, and belatedly reading the small print on the city's green and white street signs, we made a few U-turns, but it was still daylight when we finally pulled up against the curb in front of Kathy's house.

We prayed once more and got out of the car. Knowing the Holy Spirit would guide us—but not knowing what to expect—we somehow made it up the sidewalk and steps to Kathy's front porch. I pressed the button and we heard the faint sound of the doorbell ringing. It's hard to say whether we were happy or sorry when we heard footsteps on the floor inside and a woman opened the door.

Because they add a softer touch, the women on the teams were supposed to do the introductions. It was up to me.

"Are you Kathy?" I asked. She nodded. "I'm Carol, and this is, um, Bob, and this is, um, Richard. We're from Great Hills Baptist Church."

Kathy hesitated. "I would love to invite you in," she said, "but I went to the dentist for a procedure today, and I don't feel much like visiting."

A phone rang in the background.

"And you really don't need to come back. I visited your church, but I've joined Grace Covenant Church," she said quickly, turning to answer the phone and closing the door.

Having heard that Grace Covenant was a good, Bible-teaching church, we trudged back toward the car, deflated that our first visit was a dud.

But before we were halfway down the sidewalk, Kathy opened the door and called out, "Come back, there's someone else you need to talk to."

We turned around to see a woman wearing sweats splashed with red, white, and blue stars and stripes. She was headed across the grass from the house next door. Kathy came out and introduced us to her neighbor, Rebecca, who—by the way—had been on the other end of that ringing phone.

They filled us in on some background. Rebecca was Jewish. Some months before, her troubled marriage had ended in divorce. She had moved in with her aunt, who lived in the house next door to Kathy. As a friendship developed between the two neighbors, Kathy had begun to tell Rebecca about Jesus. She had even taken her to church.

When she was married, Rebecca had hungered for a closer relationship with God. She thought she could find that relationship by traveling to Israel to study with a certain Rabbi, but her husband had prevented her from going. But now, through her new friendship with Kathy, she was beginning to understand God's promise of a personal relationship with Him through Jesus, the true Messiah.

"I've been spoon-feeding the New Testament to Rebecca," Kathy said. "She's at a precarious stage of knowing who Jesus is. I think it's too soon for her to hear the gospel message."

However, thinking that anybody who was intent on drawing closer to God (as Rebecca obviously was) simply must know the heart of the gospel message, I couldn't see why she shouldn't hear it right then.

"We have to share F.A.I.T.H. with her!" I blurted.

I tend to talk before I really think things through. How was I to know if Bob, our team leader, even knew the F.A.I.T.H. outline and all those scriptures? After all, he had just been through the crash course. And with fair amounts of gray hairs among the black ones, he looked like his brain might be just as old as mine was. Maybe things weren't sticking as well as they used to for him either. But I couldn't take it back.

"I think so, too," Richard was saying.

"She is hungry for God," Bob agreed.

"Maybe you're right," Kathy conceded.

Rebecca was nodding vigorously.

So, Bob spelled out F.A.I.T.H. Pointing to the fingers on his right hand, he went through the letters and the scriptures. The F is for forgiveness: We can't get into heaven without God's forgiveness. A is for available: This forgiveness is available to everyone, but it's not automatic. The I is for impossible: It's impossible for God to allow sin in heaven. T is for turn: We must turn from our way to God's way (repent) and turn to Jesus, who died to pay for our sins and rose again. And this decision takes us to the H, which stands for heaven: Eternal life with God.

Bob included all of the scriptures, even the long T section, with only a little prompting from Richard, who had the F.A.I.T.H. outline card ready, just in case.

Finishing the verses, Bob asked, "Do you want to put your faith and trust in Jesus?"

"Yes!" Rebecca answered.

Explaining that F.A.I.T.H. could also stand for Forsaking All I Trust Him, Bob told her that she could say a simple prayer, admitting her sins, asking God for forgiveness, believing Jesus died to pay for her own personal sins and that He rose again, and asking Him to make her the person He would have her be.

"Do you want to pray with me right now?" Bob asked.

Again, she simply said, "Yes."

Hand-in-hand in the fading light, we stood in a circle in Kathy's front yard as Bob prayed and Rebecca repeated each phrase. At a point in the middle, he stopped.

Not knowing if Bob was having difficulty remembering what to pray, or if he was losing his composure, I added a line to the prayer, and Rebecca prayed after me. Bob recovered and prayed the last few lines, with Rebecca echoing each phrase in a steady voice.

As she said "Amen," Rebecca dissolved into tears. She kept apologizing, but we assured her that, though it isn't the important part, emotion often overwhelms people as they receive God's priceless gift of forgiveness, their sin debt paid in full by Jesus, and a new life with Him.

"I'll continue our Bible studies," said Kathy, her cheeks also wet with tears. Rebecca smothered all of us with hugs; then our little F.A.I.T.H. team headed for the car, almost bursting with the kind of joy that makes a person want to do back flips or yell.

We restrained ourselves from doing the back flips. And we didn't yell—until we had driven a full block from Kathy's house. Then my car shook with our commotion, emotion, and laughter.

When he could finally talk, Richard said, "Just think, this celebration is just a small taste of the one that's going on in heaven over Rebecca, a lost soul who is now found!"

This was the joy of my first experience of being personally involved when someone was born again. And the satisfaction has been just as soul filling every time since.

> *Men and brethren, sons of the family of Abraham, and those among you who fear God, to you the word of this salvation has been sent.* (Acts 13:26 NKJV)

> *For Jews request a sign, and Greeks seek after wisdom; but we preach Christ crucified, to the Jews a stumbling block and to the Greeks foolishness, but to those who are called, both Jews and Greeks, Christ the power of God and the wisdom of God.* (1 Corinthians 1:24 NKJV)

If you haven't experienced one of those celebrations, what are you waiting for? Commit the F.A.I.T.H. outline and scriptures to memory so you can easily share them. Or simply read the pages with someone—soon. Do you know someone who is trying to get closer to God but doesn't have enough information to start a relationship with Him? Write down some names and start praying for them. Then ask the Holy Spirit for His power and ask them the key question.

Breaking the Stage Fright

By about the twelfth week of the first fifteen-week F.A.I.T.H. semester, I had practiced my transitions and scriptures a lot with Chuck. I had also rehearsed them during team time with my team leader, Bob, who always held me to a correct rendering, not a hurried paraphrase. Even though I had doubted my ability to learn the whole F.A.I.T.H. outline and scriptures, God's hand was in it, and I was actually getting the whole thing down. Bob thought I was ready to share it with somebody else.

That Monday night, Burt and Sara answered the door when our F.A.I.T.H. team rang their bell. They invited us into their beautiful home, and we quickly learned that they were regular church and Sunday school attendees at Great Hills. Wanting to approach them carefully because they could do all that church stuff and still not have committed their lives to Christ, Bob asked, "Would it be okay if Carol practiced her F.A.I.T.H. presentation on you?"

"Of course," they said. "We have been curious about this program Pastor Lewis has been talking about on Sunday mornings."

I was ready, and, because God was in on it, I wasn't even nervous. I started with the key question: "In your personal opinion, what do you understand it takes for a person to go to heaven?"

I paused while they gave perfect answers, saying that they had repented of their sins, asked God for forgiveness, believed that Jesus died on the cross to pay for their sins and rose again, and had made Him their Lord and Savior.

"That's exactly right!" Bob said. "It's nice to know you'll be going to heaven with us." He paused for a minute and asked, "Would it be okay if Carol continues through the rest of the presentation for practice?"

"Sure," they said. "We would love to hear it."

Surprising myself, I breezed right through it, not even stumbling or fumbling on the hardest part, the T for turn, with all those long scriptures.

It was the perfect way to break my stage fright. I had done it, and with continuing practice—even now I sometimes go through it when I'm driving—I can always count on having the reason for the hope that is within me right on the tip of my tongue.

You may be wondering, as I was, why in the world our F.A.I.T.H. team was knocking on a door where the people were regular church attendees and already knew the Lord. Here's what Pastor told me: "We are also visiting to see if our members need prayers or just a friendly touch." He called those "ministry visits." I came to love those visits as much as salvation visits. We always assigned a team member to ask if a person or family had any prayer requests, and we prayed with them for those often-surprising needs right on the spot. These prayers, and the love they demonstrated, also opened doors for conversations about Jesus.

> Jesus said: *Again I say to you that if two of you agree on earth concerning anything that they ask, it will be done for them by My Father in heaven. For where two or three are gathered together in My name, I am there in the midst of them.* (Matthew 18:19 NKJV)

Do you know someone who could use a prayer? Maybe you've seen someone at work who seems to be down. Or maybe it will be someone you encounter when you are shopping or playing sports. This week, take the time to ask them specifically what to pray. And pray with them right on the spot. If that someone is a non-believer, he or she may just ask you how you have such faith and peace. Then you can tell them about Jesus.

Four Guys on a Sidewalk

Several F.A.I.T.H. semesters later, I was fifty-something, my friend Peggy was close to seventy, and a man named Dallas, our substitute team member that evening, also had more white hairs than black. The three of us went out from our church as a F.A.I.T.H. team one Monday night in late spring, looking like an AARP magazine cover.

We elected Dallas to drive and climbed into our seats in his SUV, praying for travel mercies, cleansing forgiveness, the Holy Spirit's guidance, and divine appointments.

God didn't disappoint us.

Our three-ring F.A.I.T.H. binder had details and driving directions for a couple of possible visits. We picked the top one and prayed for a divine appointment. With Peggy reading the computer-generated directions aloud, Dallas steered out of the church parking lot and along Austin streets. We enjoyed the fellowship on the way and arrived in the subdivision in what seemed like no time.

Climbing out of the car into the balmy Austin evening, we headed up the sidewalk to a front door. The page in our binder had given us descriptions of a fifty-something couple who had attended our church's Christmas Pageant— we'll call them Anthony and Mary—and we were ready for God to work inside that house.

I rang the doorbell, all set to make the introductions. Through the glass panes and some lacy curtains, we could see a tiny dog on the other side of the door.

In its efforts to get us off the porch, it was having a barking hissy fit. But no people stirred. We rang the bell one more time, setting off yet another outburst of high-pitched barking. Still no Anthony or Mary.

Discouraged, but not defeated, we did as the dog had demanded and returned to our car, resettling in our seats and consulting our F.A.I.T.H. notebook for the next stop. After checking the directions for a home that seemed to be a long way to go from where we were, Dallas drove up the street and made a U-turn at a T intersection at the end of the block.

As Dallas finished the U, we passed four black guys, who appeared to be in their late teens, standing on the sidewalk in front of a house.

Having no idea what God might have in mind, I remembered the printed survey cards in our binder. "Let's ask if they'll do an opinion poll," I said.

Without any hesitation, Dallas stopped the car. Getting out and approaching the young men, he asked, "Would you mind answering a few questions about church?"

Did I mention that the three of us were white and old and the boys were young and black? We had no idea how the kids would react to us. Anyway, in spite of all my Holy-Spirit-fueled optimism, I have to admit that I anticipated a speedy or emphatic "No."

But I underestimated God.

All four guys said, "Sure."

Peggy and I joined Dallas on the sidewalk with the young men, and we all exchanged names. Then, as team leader that night, half expecting at least one of the guys to walk away, I started asking the questions on the card:

"Do you think people go to church as much as they used to?"

"Why do people go to church?"

"What would you like to find in a church you would attend?"

In spite of my doubts, each of the four wanted to answer each question. Peggy wrote down what they said on a blank card, and I finally got to the last and most important survey question: "In your personal opinion, what do you understand it takes for a person to go to heaven?"

Each young man thought carefully and gave an answer. But none of the answers, which were variations of "I am a good person," matched what the Bible says.

"Would you like to know how the Bible answers that question?" I asked.

The boys still weren't looking for a way out. Their unanimous answer was "Yes."

"The Bible says it's all based on faith," I said, putting out my hand and spelling out the five letters of F.A.I.T.H. on my fingers. Using the scriptures that go with each letter, I told them the gospel message. They all listened attentively. Even when another young man drove up in a driveway across the street and waived at them, giving one or all of them a perfect excuse to split from this trio of old people, not one of them walked away. They barely even looked away.

I made it through to the H, which stands for heaven, and they were still with me, answering the questions I asked them as we went along, even asking a few questions of their own.

"F.A.I.T.H. can also stand for Forsaking All I Trust Him," I said. They nodded.

Then I asked them the most important question, "Would you like to pray with us to trust Christ as your personal Savior?" God's work again astonished me. Instead of walking away, each of the four answered "Yes."

So, standing on the sidewalk in front of one guy's house, not caring if anyone else was watching, the four young men grabbed hands and bowed their heads. Praying after me, they asked God for forgiveness, acknowledged Jesus' death for their sins and His resurrection, and invited Him into their lives, making Him their Lord and Savior and turning their lives over to Him.

They echoed "Amen" and spontaneously hugged us. Then Dallas spoke up. Besides being a willing driver, willing to make U-turns, and willing to stop to share the love of Jesus with anyone along the way, Dallas was God's divine substitute on our team for another reason. Handing each young man his business card, Dallas said, "Here's my phone number. My son is about your age, and we live near here. If you call me, we'll come by and pick you up on our way to church this Sunday."

One of them actually took him up on it, riding to church with Dallas and his son several Sundays. Six months later, the young man made another promise to God. He and his fiancée got married in our church.

For I am not ashamed of the gospel of Christ, for it is the power of God to salvation for everyone who believes,…" (Romans 1:16 NKJV)

We can only imagine what heaven is going to be like. But I have a feeling that all the unlikely suspects we have approached with the

gospel will come up to us and say, "Thank you! I'm so glad you didn't chicken out because you thought you were too old or too white or too black or too young. I'm here because you weren't afraid or ashamed to tell me the good news about Jesus Christ." Write down a few times when you have chickened out and ask God to give you the boldness to speak out the very next time an opportunity comes up.

A Fishing Trip—Two Men and a Truck

One mild and clear October evening, Chuck was driving me home from work. As we rolled to a stop at a busy commercial intersection where we would usually turn right onto the street where we lived, I happened to glance at a parking lot on our left and saw a man peering under the hood of a big old pickup. Another man sat in the front seat.

"Fish!" I said to Chuck, pointing at the men.

Jesus told the disciples He would make them fishers of men. Taking F.A.I.T.H. to the streets meant that the Holy Spirit would continue to give us fish, even on nights other than our church's Monday F.A.I.T.H. visit nights. It was our job to obey when He pointed them out. So Chuck made a right turn, then a U-turn, and pulled up beside the truck in the otherwise empty parking lot.

Chuck got out to see if he could help with the truck. I stayed in the car and prayed for the men to have open hearts and minds and for Chuck to follow the Holy Spirit's guidance.

I could just hear the men's conversation. The truck's headlights had been blinking on and off, a state of affairs that was likely to lead to a discussion with a police officer. The driver was trying to fix it first. His buddy remained in the passenger seat. It was almost dark out, and the first man was having trouble seeing the connections under the hood. Chuck came back to our car to get the flashlight we kept in the trunk.

Pointing the beam of light into the engine, they jiggled some wires, and finally the lights shone brightly and steadily. "It's just like the light of Christ in our lives," Chuck said. Then he asked, "In your personal opinion, what do you understand it takes for a person to go to heaven?"

Standing on the driver's side of the truck, the first man answered, "Jesus died to pay for my sins, and He is my personal Savior."

The second man was still sitting in the passenger seat, so Chuck went around the truck and asked him the same question through the open window.

"That's funny," the man said, "you're the third person that has asked me something about God this week. My friend here has been talking to me about my salvation for a long time. I don't know...." He paused and began again, "I don't know if I'm ready. I'm struggling."

"What's keeping you from committing your life to Christ right now?" Chuck asked.

The man shrugged.

"I could tell you what the Bible says about this," Chuck said. "Do you want to hear it?"

"Sure," the man answered. "Go ahead."

"The Bible says it's all based on faith," Chuck said. And while I continued to pray, he shared the F.A.I.T.H. outline and scriptures with the man through the open window of the truck. I could hear most of what they said. And I could see the man nodding his agreement.

When Chuck finished telling the good news about Christ, I heard the man say, "I know God has been looking for me for a long time. I guess I was looking for Him, too, since He sent all these people to help me find Him. And now you're here."

Chuck asked if he wanted to pray to confess his sins, to ask for forgiveness, to admit that Christ died to pay for his sins, that He rose again, and to declare Christ's Lordship over his life. The man nodded. His friend, who was standing just behind Chuck, said, "I'll pray with you." So the three men prayed, with Chuck saying a phrase at a time, the others repeating after him.

At the end of the prayer, the man jumped out of the truck and threw his arms around Chuck and his friend.

"I have praying for him for years, for this very thing to happen," the friend said.

I could see bright tears in the eyes of all three men.

And that's what happens when we're tuned in to the Holy Spirit's urgings to go fishing. Because we obeyed His call, the two men drove off with unblinking lights on the road and with the light of Jesus in both of their hearts.

*Then Jesus said to them, "Follow Me, and I will make you become fishers of men."
They immediately left their nets and followed Him.* (Mark 1:17–18 NKJV)

**Jesus didn't tell the disciples to become fishers of men, He said He
would make them become fishers of men. Are you ready to start fishing?
Write down some likely fishing places in your neck of the woods.**

_____

_____

Laundromat "Date"

When Chuck was a full-time, stay-at-home artist, and I was working full
time, he had been doing all of our laundry for several years. You're thinking,
what a very nice husband, aren't you? Well, of course that's true. He is a very
nice husband.

Eventually, with God's powerful intervention, Chuck's art sales started to
flourish, and he encouraged me to retire from full-time work so I could write.
The first dreaded washday Thursday after I retired, Chuck invited me to go
with him to the laundromat.

I knew this was not an attractive invitation. We were going to a hot room full
of little kids hitting earsplitting high notes and chasing each other. We would
cram our dirty clothes into at least ten washers—some of which wouldn't
work. Then we would wait through wash, rinse, and spin cycles. And we
would wipe sweat off our foreheads while we watched our clothes tumble
through the round glass of dryer doors. But I accepted this "date" anyway.

The laundromat met my expectations: washers sloshing through wash and
rinse and banging through spin cycles, three- and five-year olds running and
screaming. Thirty dryers added ten degrees to the summer atmosphere wafting in
through doors propped open with bricks. All this played against the background
of a TV talk show, where everyone was yelling at once—in Spanish.

But I was having fun anyway. Waiting for the wash cycle to finish, I gave
gospel tracts to all the frazzled moms, who struggled to keep the kids from
climbing into a dryer or tearing up the snack machine. And I handed them
to each of the stoic men, who silently came in, did one load of laundry, and
left as quickly as possible. I asked them "Spanish or English?" They picked
one and said, "Thank you." Most started reading the tracts. After all, there

wasn't much else to do, and the little pieces of paper offered some very good news.

A woman came in, pretty, blonde and perhaps in her mid thirties. Though she didn't have any kids with her, she looked tired beyond her years. She put in quarters and soap and stuffed her laundry into several machines then slumped onto a bench to wait. I put a tract in her hand. She looked up, brightened briefly, and said "Thank you."

Folding hot clothes as Chuck took them out of the dryers, I had almost forgotten about the blonde woman. But the Holy Spirit had drawn Chuck's attention to her. Packing the last of our fresh-smelling laundry into pillowcases, he said, "Go talk to that lady. She hasn't even moved since you gave her the tract."

While Chuck gathered up the pillowcases full of clothes and took them to the car, I went over to the woman. "Hi, I'm Carol," I said.

She looked up and said, "Hi, I'm Susie."

I wasn't sure how to start, so I ventured, "If you don't already have a church, I'd like to invite you to come to our church. The address is on the back of that paper."

"It's very nice of you to come over and talk to me," she answered. "I'm having a tough day."

"God loves you," I said.

"He does?" she said.

"If you died today," I asked, "would you go to heaven?"

"I don't think so," she answered.

"Would you like to be sure you're going to heaven?" I asked.

"Of course," was the reply.

So, oblivious to the ongoing clamor of the laundromat, I shared the F.A.I.T.H. outline and Bible verses—which somehow remained lodged in my gray head—with Susie. Her blue eyes met mine, and she nodded her head in agreement with every verse, sitting up straighter and beginning to show real signs of life.

As I got to the H, which stands for heaven, I recited the verses where Jesus says, "*I have come that they may have life, and that they may have it more abundantly.*" (John 10:10b, NKJV) and where He says, "*And if I go and prepare a place for you,*"

I will come again and receive you to Myself; that where I am, there you may be also." (John 14:3, NKJV). Then I asked Susie if she would like to give her life to Jesus, trusting Him alone for her salvation and receiving His gift of forgiveness.

"Yes," she said. So, in the middle of the laundromat's chaos, Susie prayed after me: "Heavenly Father, I am a sinner, and I need a Savior. I believe Jesus died for my sins, and He rose from the dead. Please forgive me, Jesus. Take over my life, and make me the person you want me to be. Thank you, Jesus. Amen."

She looked up at me, beaming with joy and saying, "Thank you! Thank you!" I told her it was all God's doing and the blessing I received was so full that I should be thanking her. Then I repeated my invitation to come to our church some time. She assured me she would try. I showed her the back of the tract, where it says to start a relationship with God by going to church, praying every day, and reading the Bible—starting with the book of John, which would help her understand who Jesus is, then Acts and Romans, then the rest of the New Testament, and finally, the Old Testament.

I hugged her and walked outside to the car, where, knowing exactly what I was doing, Chuck was waiting and praying patiently. He also understood that my happy face had nothing to do with the fact that laundry day was over. He knew it was the sheer pleasure of being there when Susie was born again.

> *This same good news that came to you is going out all over the world. It is bearing fruit everywhere by changing lives, just as it changed your lives from the day you first heard and understood the truth about God's wonderful grace.* (Colossians 1:6 NLT)

Have you ever experienced that joy? Look around as you go through each day. God will give you people to talk to, people who need your attention, your touch, your prayers, and the forgiveness only Jesus can give. Write down a few places you go regularly, and start to think of them as places to notice those people. They may even be standing or sitting on the edges of your church.

God Can Use Us—Even When We're Cranky

Chuck was almost home after a long summer day of errands in the tangle of traffic and interminable stoplights that is Austin, Texas. As his last errand, he planned to return a car part he had bought by mistake. Almost to the Pep Boys automotive store, he discovered that he had forgotten to take the part along. He headed back home to get it—cranky! And, seemingly, not in tune with the Holy Spirit.

However, the Holy Spirit was in tune with Chuck. Eastbound on Oltorf Street just past Interstate 35, Chuck happened to notice a security guard sitting on a bench, taking a break in the shade next to the La Quinta hotel.

The Holy Spirit said, *"Go talk to him."*

I'm tired and cranky. Maybe some other time, Chuck thought.

Ignoring Chuck's mood, the Holy Spirit didn't let up. *"Go talk to him."*

Well, here's the deal, Chuck offered, *I'll go home and get the part, and if he's still there when I get back, I'll talk to him.*

He drove the few blocks home, got the car part, and headed back toward Pep Boys, passing the La Quinta again. The guy was still sitting on the same bench. So Chuck parked the car and walked across the parking lot to the man. He was nervous but conscious of the fact that God does all the work if we just step out in obedience.

"Hello," he said. "Hot, isn't it?"

"Yes, it is," the man said.

"You probably don't have much time left on your break," Chuck started, "so I'll get right to the point. In your personal opinion, what do you think it takes for a person to go to heaven?"

The man thought for a minute, then answered, "I honestly don't know."

"Would you like to hear what the Bible says?" Chuck asked.

"Sure," the man answered.

So Chuck shared the F.A.I.T.H. outline and scriptures, and was elated when the man wanted to pray—right there on that bench, taking a break in the shade—to invite Christ into his life.

Chuck explained that it was simply a matter of telling God he was sorry for his sins, that he knew he needed a savior, that he believed Jesus died for his sins and rose again, and that he was committing his life to Jesus.

Instead of waiting for Chuck to lead him in the prayer, the man simply bowed his head and started talking aloud to God. Chuck bowed his head, too.

When they both looked up, the man said, "Thank you so much! You have changed my life. You wouldn't believe the mess I have made of things at home. I feel like a brand new man, really able to go home and make things right again."

"It was God who changed your life, not me, but the rest is exactly right," Chuck answered. "Here's what the Bible says: *'If anyone is in Christ, he is a new creature. Old things pass away, and all things become new.'*"

After a hug and a bunch more thank-yous, the man went back to work, smiling.

And Chuck headed for Pep Boys, also smiling, and thanking God for letting him participate in the spiritual birth of a brand new baby Christian—even when he was cranky.

> *The Lord gave this message to Jonah son of Amittai: "Get up and go to the great city of Nineveh. Announce my judgment against it because I have seen how wicked its people are." But Jonah got up and went in the opposite direction to get away from the Lord. He went down to the port of Joppa, where he found a ship leaving for Tarshish. He bought a ticket and went on board, hoping to escape from the Lord by sailing to Tarshish.* (Jonah 1:1–3 NLT)

After a storm came up and the sailors threw Jonah overboard, he ended up in the belly of a fish. Three days later, he made it to the beach.

> *Then the Lord spoke to Jonah a second time: "Get up and go to the great city of Nineveh, and deliver the message I have given you." This time Jonah obeyed the Lord's command and went to Nineveh, a city so large that it took three days to see it all. On the day Jonah entered the city, he shouted to the crowds: "Forty days from now Nineveh will be destroyed!" The people of Nineveh believed God's message, and from the greatest to the least, they declared a fast and put on burlap to show their sorrow.* (Jonah 3:3–5 NLT)

Are you on the lookout for God's appointments? _____ Are you willing to obey? Even when you're reluctant? Or cranky?_____

God Also Works in Spanish

As Chuck steered the car into the HalfPrice Books parking lot, he passed a Kobe Japanese Steakhouse. He couldn't help but notice six men sitting on the curb, waiting.

Chuck felt the Holy Spirit's nudge, *"Go talk to them."*

Considering himself to be a full-time evangelist (as God calls all of us to be), Chuck was ready to answer God's call anytime, anywhere. He knew the F.A.I.T.H. outline and scriptures, and he had gospel tracts in his wallet. But this time he started to get shy. After all, there were six of them.

They'll be gone before I can get over there, he argued, parking the car in front of the bookstore and heading for the door.

Inside, his eyes already scanning the bookshelves, he heard the Holy Spirit again, *"Go talk to them."*

Unable to say no to a second call, Chuck walked back outside and saw the six men still sitting on the curb. Whispering a prayer for the Holy Spirit's guidance and taking a big breath, he walked over to them.

"Hi, I'm Chuck," he began.

"I'm Carlos," one of them said in a heavy Spanish accent, "we're waiting for the boss to open the door so we can go to work. He's late."

Realizing he didn't have much time, Chuck forged ahead, saying, "If you died today, would you go to heaven?"

Carlos was sure. "No, I would go to hell," he said.

Though it was a Japanese restaurant, all of the men were Hispanic. Besides Carlos, only two of them understood English. Unruffled by this, Chuck asked Carlos to help with translation. They asked the other men about their chances of going to heaven. They had no idea.

"Would you like to know how you can go to heaven?" Chuck asked. Carlos repeated the question. They all nodded.

Feeling his inadequacies for this task, and asking the Holy Spirit to take over, Chuck pulled a gospel tract out of his pocket. With Carlos (the man who said he was going to hell) translating, Chuck read the scriptures, explaining the need for forgiveness because of the problem of sin. They relayed the good news: the availability of forgiveness because of God's love for us. They explained that forgiveness is not automatic because it's impossible for God to allow our sin into heaven, but that we have the option of turning from sin, personally accepting Christ's death on the cross as payment for all of our sins, and believing in His resurrection. They talked about the hope of an eternity in heaven.

Still unsure when the boss might show up, and uptight about having to pause for Carlos to repeat each bit in Spanish, Chuck practically shouted, "Each person has to decide!" Then, as quickly as he could, he explained that it is a one-time commitment: admitting sins to God, asking Him for forgiveness, understanding that Christ died for each of us and came back from death, trusting Him alone for our salvation and not our works, and giving Him Lordship over our lives.

"Would any of you like to pray with me right now?" he asked. Carlos nodded vigorously. Then he repeated the question for the others.

The rest of them also nodded and then bowed their heads. Chuck prayed a few words at a time in English, echoed first by Carlos in Spanish, then by the other men as they invited Jesus into their lives.

With his loud "Amen" at the end with the others, Carlos could no longer say he was going to hell.

Chuck was hugging the men and celebrating their newfound promise of a Savior and heaven when the boss walked up and opened the restaurant door, calling the new Christians to go to work. Chuck headed back to the bookstore, praising God and shaking his head in joyful amazement.

> *For as the rain comes down, and the snow from heaven, and do not return there, but water the earth, and make it bring forth and bud, that it may give seed to the sower and bread to the eater, so shall My word be that goes forth from My mouth; it shall not return to Me void, but it shall accomplish what I please, and it shall prosper in the thing for which I sent it. For you shall go out with joy, and be led out with peace; the mountains and the hills shall break forth into singing before you, and all the trees of the field shall clap their hands.* (Isaiah 55:10–11 NKJV)

God's Word doesn't come back empty but is sure to bring joy. Where can you test it yourself?

Chapter 5

Mission NYC

If you make yourself available to share the good news about Jesus, God will let you know where He wants you to go. In addition to the fields ripe for spiritual harvest right where you live, He may call you to go somewhere else for a short time—or for a long time. As was true when God called someone in the Bible, the assignment may not be what you expect. But He's always clear about it.

In the spring of 2004, we joined the Pastor's Class, the new members' class at Great Hills. Though Michael Lewis was the new and extremely busy senior pastor at the six-thousand-member church, he taught the class himself.

One Sunday, Mickey, who kept our class paperwork in order and made the announcements each week, invited all one hundred of us to a Pastor's Class Social. It would be a pool party, desserts only. The entertainment would be Danny Souder of Strategic Mission Partners Global, who was to talk about an upcoming mission trip to New York City.

I was sure this pool party idea wouldn't tempt Chuck, not even with desserts involved. We're both health nuts; we haven't been seen in swimsuits for years; and he's certainly not a party animal. But he stunned me with what could only have been God's work.

"Let's go," he said. "I want to hear about that New York trip."

So, on a warm Saturday afternoon in June, we packed up a dozen of my healthy homemade oatmeal cookies and drove to the address in the cedar- and live-oak-covered hills west of Austin. We found ourselves ringing the doorbell of a limestone-clad mansion. Against our better judgment, we sampled some incredibly delicious lemon bars and brownies as we leaned against granite kitchen countertops and mingled with twenty or so of the Pastor's Class members. Eventually, we wandered outside toward chairs set in rows on a shady terrace above the swimming pool.

I was about to sit down when I noticed that Pastor's three girls, Charity, Faith, and Hope, and Debbie and Darrel's son, Nicolas, were still in the pool, giggling, splashing, and shrieking as six-to-ten-year-olds do in swimming pools.

Seeing no grown-ups near the pool, I wandered down some limestone steps to watch the kids. They were taking turns paddling across the pool on an inflated dinosaur. Arriving at the other side, each kid would give up the dinosaur and swim back to the other side. On her first attempt, Pastor's youngest, six-year-old Hope, made it across the pool with the dinosaur. However, her version of swimming back took her hand-over-hand along the ledge of flat stones at the end of the pool—the deep end. As she was making her way across, I noticed a two-foot gap in the stones where a landscaped waterfall spilled into the pool.

Hearing the Lord's prompting, I edged over to stand near that gap to see what would happen. Sure enough, when Hope's little hand reached out to grab the next handhold on the side of the pool, it grabbed nothing. She went right under.

I slipped my hand into the water and caught her hand, swinging her over to the next spot where she could continue on her way to the other side.

"Thank you, Lord," I whispered.

I don't think anyone, including Hope, realized what had happened. The adults were engrossed in Danny's NYC talk, and the other kids were still giggling and shrieking at the other end of the pool.

The only thing was, in answering God's call to help Hope, I had missed hearing about the NYC mission. But Chuck heard about it.

God's work in Chuck's life always surprises me. He's done it a lot, so I shouldn't be so surprised. It's just that Chuck is a loner. He's not exactly unsociable, but he doesn't like meeting people. I guess you might call him a social introvert.

Who would have thought Chuck would want to drive three hours to meet a bunch of Christian strangers at the Dallas/Ft. Worth airport, board a plane, endure a long stopover at Chicago O'Hare, board another plane, climb on a bus that would take us from LaGuardia Airport to bunk beds in a dorm room at New York's Pace University, share the gospel with the strangers of New York for a week, and then do the travel maneuvers in reverse? Well, he did.

> *With men this is impossible, but with God all things are possible.* (Mathew 19:26 NKJV)

Later that summer, as the only ones from our church to answer God's call to New York City, Chuck and I drove from Austin to DFW International Airport and flew to New York for a week with our leader, Danny, and eighteen men and women from Dallas-area churches.

The focus of the mission was to invite New Yorkers to Mosaic Manhattan Church, a newly planted church. For the time, the church was meeting in an elementary school a few blocks from the edge of Ground Zero, which in 2004 was still a vast crater where the World Trade Center Towers had stood before September 11, 2001.

> Jesus said to Nicodemus: *For God so loved the world that He gave His only begotten Son, that whoever believes in Him should not perish but have everlasting life. For God did not send His Son into the world to condemn the world, but that the world through Him might be saved.* (John 3:16–17 NKJV)

As you read these stories, keep in mind that you don't have to go to Russia, China, Brazil, Africa, or even NYC. The mission field begins right outside your door. And sometimes it's even inside that door.

Where is your mission field?

Let Them Eat Donuts

We had arrived in New York City for God's mission. After spending Sunday night on hard bunk beds in Pace University dorm rooms, the twenty-member mission team, feeling like a bunch of ducklings trying not to scatter, followed Danny Souder through the canyons of Manhattan. We waited for walk lights, dodged taxicabs, and squeezed between pedestrians who were rushing down the city's sidewalks to work. Shaded by floors and floors of offices above, we caught whiffs of bacon, eggs, coffee, and pizza as we passed street-level coffee shops and delis, stores packed with boom boxes and TVs, and windows decorated with shoes, shirts, slacks, and dresses.

Finally, Danny led us into a narrow side street, the darkest block of all. The only hints of life were racks of postcards, sunglasses, and Statue of Liberty miniatures outside a tiny storefront. Above them, the buildings seemed to meet as they rose toward the sky above us. The doors looked like the places where dreadful gangsters meet the unsuspecting good guys in movies—just before kidnappings, shootings, and car chases.

Promptly at eight A.M., one of the doors opened.

Instead of dreadful gangsters, however, a man, whose joyful smile practically lit up that dark block, came out. "Hi everyone," he said. "I'm Rick. Thanks for coming."

Right away, he began to answer our unasked questions. "I'm not the pastor. I'm a volunteer at Mosaic Manhattan Church. I know what you're thinking," he added, glancing toward the shadowy doorway. "This isn't the church building. On Sundays we meet at PS89, an elementary school near Ground Zero." During the week, kids go to school in that building, so we've rented office space here. Come on in."

En masse, we climbed three steps and walked through the door. Practically filling the small lobby, we were surprised to find ourselves surrounded by the elaborate marble and brass decor of a hundred-year-old office building. Then we couldn't help but notice stacks of Krispy Kreme donut boxes in a corner.

"Yep, they're really donuts," Rick volunteered, guessing what we were thinking again. "You're going to be on street corners, passing out donuts—with postcards that invite people to our church."

We had heard of mission teams passing out water, rice, wheat, and beans. But donuts?

Whatever the chores, we had come to serve the new church. So we grabbed some Krispy Kreme boxes and, in teams of twos and fours, we spread out to nearby street corners. Chuck and I soon found ourselves saying, "Good morning, would you like a free donut?" to New Yorkers climbing up out of subways and down from buses.

You wouldn't think it would be hard to get rid of six or eight dozen donuts, but most of the commuters kept walking, looking at us as if they thought we had lost our minds. I suppose they were as suspicious of our friendly smiles and Texas accents as they were of our motives. Or maybe they were watching their figures.

However, some commuters had no such reservations. We handed each of those a donut, a napkin, and a postcard invitation to the church, repeating, "We hope you'll come to church sometime soon." A few asked for two donuts, one for a friend at the office. We gave them two, but only if they promised to give the friend a postcard, too.

Eventually the Krispy Kreme boxes were empty. We stuffed them in trashcans and found our way back to the shadowy street to see what other chores Rick had for us.

He gave us plastic bags, saying we were to gather up trash as we walked along our assigned streets. In theory, this service ministry was meant to draw questions, such as, "Why in the world are you picking up trash on a New York street?" The questions would allow us to share our faith and our postcards. Maybe the New Yorkers weren't curious, however, or maybe they were reluctant to get involved with strangers. Anyway, nobody asked.

We suspected a secondary motive for this assignment: to pick up any wayward postcards from the hundreds we had passed out with the donuts. We only found one of those postcards, and, surprisingly, the sidewalks of New York didn't have much other trash either.

After the allotted hour of trash collection, we were to prayer walk for an hour. This meant praying for all the people on the streets and in the buildings. Then we were to eat lunch and meet at a nearby park to pass out cookies.

We did this routine for two days. On Wednesday and Thursday, we changed to granola bars instead of donuts and cookies. God supplied the perfect New York weather, and we supplied the willing feet and hands. This side of heaven, we won't know the full outcome of the donuts, granola bars, cookies, and postcards we gave away or the trash pickup and prayer walking we did. But God knows. The following stories tell about some of the encounters with the people of New York.

After Jesus had washed the disciples' feet, He said: *You call me "Teacher" and "Lord," and you are right, because that's what I am. And since I, your Lord and Teacher, have washed your feet, you ought to wash each other's feet. I have given you an example to follow. Do as I have done to you. I tell you the truth, slaves are not greater than their master. Nor is the messenger more important than the one who sends the message. Now that you know these things, God will bless you for doing them.* (John 13:17 NLT)

Write down a few times you served the Lord by serving others—or some times when you can do it in the future.

_____

_____

Lunch at the Park

After spending the first morning of our mission trip to New York handing out Krispy Kreme donuts and postcards to Manhattan commuters, picking up trash on several blocks, and prayer walking what seemed like miles of the city, we finally took a lunch break. Then, consulting a photocopied map, we walked along the edge of Ground Zero—where the huge pieces of earth-moving equipment at the bottom of the World Trade Center excavation site looked like tiny toys—and made our way to a park where we were to meet the rest of our mission team.

We found the fenced pocket of grass, swings, slides, and benches—a cheerful oasis hemmed in by the city's concrete, bricks, steel, and glass. Taking a giant parachute, soccer balls, and Hula-hoops out of a big duffle bag, several of our teammates were rounding up about twenty little kids to play with them. At first we watched all the running and laughing, hard-pressed to distinguish the park's kids from our grown-ups.

Then it occurred to us: This playtime gave the rest of the team an opportunity to pass out packets of chocolate chip cookies and more postcards to the mommies and nannies who sat on the grass and park benches watching the kids, and to mingle with the other people in the park.

I noticed office workers on their lunch break leaning on a chest-high mesh fence and enjoying the summer day, also amused with the silliness. I can't exactly explain how He does it, but the Holy Spirit pointed out a young man in dark slacks and a white shirt. I walked up to him.

"Cute, huh?" I said, handing him one of the postcards and a packet of cookies.

"Yeah, they are," he answered.

"My name is Carol, what's yours?" I said.

"Manny," he said, taking a bite out of his sandwich.

Figuring he would probably have to go back to work soon, I didn't waste any time. "In your personal opinion," I blurted, "what do you understand that it takes for a person to go to heaven?"

Like all but a few of the people I've asked that question, Manny didn't seem to be startled by it. And like the others, Manny thought for a minute. Swallowing his bite of sandwich, he finally came up with an answer: "Well, I've been a pretty good person."

I must say that I would have a good start on a fortune if I had a nickel for everyone who answers the question that way. At least 90 percent say that. But being a good person won't get you to heaven.

However, I didn't argue with him. Instead, I asked, "Would you like to know how the Bible answers that question?"

Having no idea how long he had left on his lunch break, I was glad when he said, "Yes, I would."

While Manny finished his sandwich, I went through the F.A.I.T.H. outline and scriptures we had learned at our church. He could have simply waited until I paused for a breath to make his getaway, using the excuse that he needed to get back to work. Instead, he listened thoughtfully, asking a few questions, paying close attention.

When I finished the last scripture, I looked straight at him and said, "Do you want to ask Jesus into your life right now?"

"You've given me a lot to think about," he said. "But I don't want to rush this decision. And I have to get back to work."

"I'm glad you're taking this seriously," I said. "When you're ready, you can pray anywhere. The prayer would just be telling God, in your own words, that you admit you're a sinner, that you believe that Jesus died for your sins, and that He has risen from the dead. Ask Him for His forgiveness. Invite Him to take over your life and make you the person He wants you to be. Then thank Him."

"Well, thank you for taking the time to explain everything to me," Manny said. Then he was walking away, crossing the park toward one of the tall buildings with a package of cookies and a postcard invitation to church in his hand.

I'm always delighted when someone allows me to share the good news. Until I get to heaven, only God knows what Manny has done with it. Since then, I've been praying for him.

> *So then faith comes by hearing, and hearing by the word of God.* (Romans 10:17 NKJV)

You will be pleasantly surprised when 1) God leads you to the Mannys in your life, 2) you speak up, and 3) they want to hear about His saving grace. As that scripture says, they can't have faith until they hear. Will you speak up? _____

He Didn't Mug Me

The young black man slouched on a bench across the street from a tiny park in Manhattan. His plaid shirt and baggy shorts looked more like PJs than clothes you would wear to an office job or a construction site. I guessed he was just hanging out. But I couldn't help but think of all those muggings in New York.

However, with the boldness that comes from being on a mission trip to the city, really taking that mission seriously, and leaning on the Holy Spirit, I went right up to him, handed him a postcard and said, "Hi, I'm Carol. I'd like to invite you to the Mosaic Church. It's right here in Manhattan."

Not revealing any of his own suspicions about this middle-aged white lady who trotted across a busy street to talk to him, he said, "Hi, I'm Tiniko."

I said something about God giving us a nice day, and he agreed. Then I asked him if he thought he would go to heaven if he died that day.

"I don't know," he said.

"Do you have time for me to share what the Bible says?" I asked. "It will only take about ten minutes."

"Okay, sure," he said, sitting up straighter.

I sat down on the bench beside him and shared the F.A.I.T.H. outline and scriptures. When I finished, I asked if he would like to pray to ask Jesus to come into his heart and life.

"Well," he said, "I'm not quite ready to take that step, and I have to go now."

"Don't wait too long," I said as he walked away, postcard in hand.

I guess I could have been disappointed, but I was elated. This young man, who could have mugged me, or just told me to get lost, had sat quietly and listened to the gospel message, and now he has some information to consider. And he has an invitation to a church.

I did the part God gave me to do. And God will do the rest.

> *And they have defeated him (Satan) by the blood of the Lamb and by their testimony. And they did not love their lives so much that they were afraid to die.* (Revelation 12:11 NLT)

He will do it for you, too. When was the last time you were bold for Jesus?

Sawdust and Tears

On another day of our mission trip to New York City, after passing out ten dozen Krispy Kreme donuts at a busy bus stop, picking up litter on about a mile of Manhattan sidewalks, and prayer walking another mile of city blocks, Chuck and I were glad when Danny, our mission team leader, suggested a lunch break. Other team members, Sue and Tim, joined the three of us at a corner deli. We ordered sandwiches at the counter and dropped tiredly into chairs around a red Formica-top table.

Unwrapping our sandwiches, we began to discuss the potential for other mission trips to New York. Suddenly, Sue got the strangest look on her face and started checking her pockets. Her expression quickly went from shock to panic. She and Tim left the table for a minute and returned. It was obvious that something was very wrong. Nothing should have been able to pry their attention away from the fat sandwiches, crunchy chips, and cold sodas on the table. But they were no longer interested in food.

"We have to go," Tim said.

Dumbfounded that they would just leave, I managed to ask, "What's wrong?"

Sue and Tim hesitated to share this trouble with us. After all, we had met only two days earlier, as the twenty-one mission team members boarded the plane to New York.

"It's okay," I offered. "We can see you're upset. We just want to pray for you."

Tim was in high-gear-frantic mode, and Sue was practically in tears, but they sat back down.

"Sue had two hundred dollars in her pocket, all we brought with us, and it's gone," Tim babbled. "We have to retrace our steps to see if she dropped it."

Fat chance it would still be there, I thought.

"If we don't find it, we'll go back to the dorm to see if maybe she left it in the room after all," he finished.

We grabbed their hands and said a quick prayer for their peace and for God to restore the money. They got up and walked away, eyes scanning the floor as they disappeared out the door.

Silently, we finished our sandwiches, finding that our focus had shifted from the conversation about future missions to the people eating lunch around us.

At a table just across from me, a husky man sat alone, his hair, sweatshirt, and jeans covered with sawdust. The Holy Spirit nudged me. *"Go talk to him."*

"Go talk to that man," I told Chuck.

"God showed him to you," he answered. "He's yours."

So, I grabbed one of the postcards and stood up. Often, by the time I make up my mind to start my approach, the person I'm heading for is going—or long gone. This time, he was still there, taking big bites out of a sandwich.

It wasn't about me. It was God's assignment. So, like strapping on a parachute before that big jump, I gathered up my courage, and walked over to him.

"Hi, I'm Carol," I said.

He said his name was Asher.

"I'd like to invite you to a new church right here in Manhattan," I continued, handing him the postcard.

"I don't go to church," he said.

I asked if he had any spiritual beliefs. He said he believed in God. I asked if he would go to heaven if he died that day.

"I don't know," he answered, biting off another chunk of bread and ham.

I asked him if he minded if I shared the Bible's answer, and he nodded for me to go ahead.

"God, your Father in heaven," I began, "loves you so much that He gave His only Son to pay for your sins."

With just that much said, I couldn't believe what I was seeing. Sitting in a New York deli on his lunch hour, this rough, tough construction worker had tears rolling through the sawdust on his cheeks.

"What's wrong," I asked.

"My father was nothing like that," he mumbled.

"I'm sorry," I said, not knowing what else to say.

"But God does love you that much," I finally added. "Is it okay if I go on?"

He could have told me to shut up. He could have said he had to get back to work. Instead, he said, "Okay."

I went through the scriptures, asking a few questions, making sure he understood. Then I asked if he wanted to pray with me to invite Jesus into his life. "I'm just not ready," he said in an unsteady voice. "It's the first time I've heard this, and I need to think. Anyway, I have to get back to work," he said, getting up and crumpling his sandwich wrapper. "But I sure do appreciate your taking the time to talk to me."

God is so good. He uses us when we're feeling shy. He even uses bad situations, like the missing money, to shift our attention, to create opportunities. He opens up rough, tough people we think would never open up.

Who would have thought this rugged man would sit and discuss his earthly father and his heavenly Father with a stranger in that New York deli? And who would have thought I had the guts to talk to him?

God would.

All we have to do is show up, ready to obey the Holy Spirit's promptings.

> *And we know that all things work together for good to those who love God, to those who are the called according to His purpose.* (Romans 8:28 NKJV)

You, too, will find out how great God is. He uses all things for good. Are you ready to obey the Holy Spirit's promptings? _____

Phil's Meat

That night, after Sue and Tim left the deli in such a frantic state, their eyes scouring the floor of the deli, miles of New York sidewalks, and every inch of their dorm room for the missing money, they eventually met the rest of our group at a restaurant in Chinatown. You probably guessed it. They hadn't found even a dollar of the lost cash. We quietly gathered up a collection for them, passing bills from hand to hand under the tablecloth. Chuck went to the restroom and counted it and came back smiling. Of course, since God was in on it, the random amounts from the group were only a few dollars short of the money they had lost.

After dinner, the team had the rest of the evening free to investigate New York. Sue and Tim said they were going back to the Pace University dorm. Chuck wanted to give them the money in a more private setting, so instead of heading to Times Square, we walked with them. Stepping off the elevator, Chuck stuffed the wadded up bills in Tim's hand. Tim and Sue laughed, cried, hugged us, and praised God, all at the same time. Then, exhausted, they went to their room.

Chuck's Chinese supper had already worn off, so he headed downstairs to see if he could find a decent snack in one of the vending machines he had seen on the main floor. Finding myself alone in our tenth-floor lobby, I plopped into an overstuffed vinyl armchair to read my Bible. I thought our mission team members were the only occupants of the tenth floor, but maybe five minutes after I sat down, the lobby elevator doors opened and a young man I didn't recognize bounced out. Waving a cellophane package, he shouted, "I caught the meat!" He must have been bursting to tell somebody how his evening had gone.

"What?" I asked.

"I was at the Letterman Show, and I caught the meat!" he said, still waving the package.

I didn't watch Letterman, and I had no idea what he was talking about. "What do you mean, you caught the meat?" I asked.

"Well," he said, "when David Letterman comes out on the stage, he tosses meat to the members of the studio audience, and I caught this."

I was thinking, *What is a guy who's staying in a dorm room going to do with meat?* But I showered him with congratulations anyway.

He could have just gone to his room, but he wasn't in a hurry to let the thrill of the moment die down, and he didn't seem to have anyone else to tell his great news.

It occurred to me that I had some even better news for him.

"So, what's your name?" I asked.

"I'm Phil," he said. "A bunch of us are here for a convention. We're all staying on this floor."

"Hi, Phil, I'm Carol, and I have a question for you," I said. "In your personal opinion, what do you understand it takes for a person to go to heaven?"

"I have no idea," he said. I asked if he wanted to hear how the Bible answers the question. "Sure," he said, leaning against a table.

Though others in our group were returning, a few at a time, filling the chairs and couches in the lobby, no one interrupted me as I shared the F.A.I.T.H. scriptures with Phil. After I finished, he had a bunch of questions. Chuck, who had come back with a bag of chips, answered some of them, and one of our team members, a pastor, answered others.

At least an hour later, Phil stood up and stretched his arms toward the ceiling, saying, "I guess it's time to head to bed. I enjoyed our discussion, but I'm not ready to commit my life to your Jesus just yet."

"I have a challenge for you," the pastor said. "I dare you to get a Bible and read the book of John—it's in the New Testament—over the next thirty days. At the end of that time, consider what we have told you, consider who Jesus was and is, and make your decision."

Phil assured us that he would take our challenge seriously and walked down the hallway, still clutching his package of meat.

That night was one of the most important of his young life. He had caught meat from a TV star, quite a treat. More importantly, he had caught the seed of a brand new life.

God gave us the thrill of planting it. It's God's job to water it. When He harvests is up to Him—and Phil.

***

Then Chuck told us about his trip downstairs, giving us another reason to celebrate. He had struck up a conversation with the security guard stationed behind a counter near the vending machine. The man was unsure about his final destination. When Chuck explained God's plan of salvation, the man prayed with him to turn his life over to Jesus!

And remember, the Lord's patience gives people time to be saved. (2 Peter 3:15 NLT)

Now may He who supplies seed to the sower, and bread for food, supply and multiply the seed you have sown and increase the fruits of your righteousness. (2 Corinthians 9:10 NKJV)

Jesus said: *You know the saying, "Four months between planting and harvest." But I say, wake up and look around. The fields are already ripe for harvest. The harvesters are paid good wages, and the fruit they harvest is people brought to eternal life. What joy awaits both the planter and the harvester alike!* (John 4:35–36 NLT)

Someone around you needs to know Jesus. God gives you plenty of seeds. What seeds have you planted lately?

_____

_____

_____

Sasquatch Sighting in Manhattan

Our New York mission trip took the twenty of us and our leader Danny all over the south end of Manhattan Island, giving out donuts, cookies, and granola bars, picking up trash, and prayer walking.

One afternoon, Sue and Tim and Chuck and I prayer walked a good part of the area of southwestern Manhattan known as Tribeca. We prayed for the people in each warehouse, office building, store, restaurant, and apartment to yearn for personal relationships with God and to trust Jesus for salvation. We wandered into a warehouse district along West Street, not too far from the waterfront, where nobody who was paying attention—and didn't have to be there—would walk. It was broad daylight, however, and we were confident in God's presence.

Coming to a vacant lot strewn with rocks, weeds, and broken concrete, we saw a tangle of lights, cameras, trucks, and people huddled around some scruffy men in sleeveless t-shirts and someone dressed up like a seven-foot Sasquatch. The sun was shining brightly, taking the temperature well above eighty degrees. Whoever was playing Sasquatch must have been roasting in that costume.

Still across the street, we stood in a circle and prayed for this odd crowd. Then, continuing to walk around the block, we ended up in the shadow of a warehouse. As my eyes adjusted, I noticed another big man in a hairy costume. He was sitting on the steps of a loading dock only twenty feet from us, no doubt grateful to be in the shade, holding the furry "head" in his hand instead of wearing it. The Holy Spirit's prodding won out over my shyness, and I walked up to him.

"Hi," I said, handing him a postcard. "Here's an invitation to a brand new church that meets in an elementary school near Ground Zero. I have to ask, what's going on here?"

"It's the Beastie Boys," he said. "They're making a rock video. I'm Sasquatch, well, the backup Sasquatch. They've been shooting with that guy all morning."

I had no idea who the Beastie Boys might be. But when I came along, here was this giant man in a Sasquatch outfit, just killing time, waiting for the chance to be in a video with them.

Sasquatch looked down at the postcard. And I found more courage. "What do you believe it takes for a person to go to heaven?" I asked.

He thought for a minute then answered, "I don't really know."

"Would you like to hear how the Bible answers that question?" I asked.

He nodded, and I was gearing up to share F.A.I.T.H. Just then, however, the backup Sasquatch got the nod from the director.

And that was it. The Holy Spirit had given me the boldness to approach a person who seriously scared me, and who I least expected to want to discuss anything about God. And the guy turned out to be open to the subject. Since I had obeyed the heavenly nudge, this tall man was at least thinking about Him.

As Sasquatch number two jammed the furry headpiece on his head and walked into the sunshine across the street, I turned him over to God to continue His work.

Chuck and I and Tim and Sue walked another block and circled up to pray again. This time we prayed specifically for the Beastie Boys, the camera crew, and Sasquatch—one and two. Our prayer was that they would somehow find the light of Jesus, and with that light, they would eventually influence many people. It's unlikely that, this side of heaven, we will find out what happened. But God is at work.

> One night the Lord spoke to Paul in a vision and told him, "Don't be afraid! Speak out! Don't be silent! For I am with you, and no one will attack and harm you, for many people in this city belong to me." (Acts 18:9–10 NLT)

When have you answered God's call to talk to somebody, in spite of your fears?

_____

_____

_____

Men in Suits Wearing Guns

Our dorm rooms at Pace University were less than a block from the Manhattan end of the Brooklyn Bridge. About a block in the other direction, we had discovered a short-order café, a great spot for breakfast. Before we went to worship at Mosaic Manhattan Church on Sunday, the last day of our weeklong mission trip, we ate breakfast at our café.

We were eating pancakes and eggs when the little bell over the front door jangled. Six men in black suits, white shirts, and dark ties came in. Unless the setting is a men's class at church, groups of men in black suits rarely gather on a Sunday morning. So, curious about them, I watched the men order and pay for their breakfasts at the counter. Then each one removed his jacket, carefully hung it on the back of a chair, and sat down at the table beside us. They might not have kept my full attention, but with those jackets off, I could see that each of the men had a holstered gun strapped across his ribcage.

Who are these men? And what are they doing in our café—with guns? Stoked with the Holy Spirit's boldness I had been tapping the whole time we had been in New York, I leaned over and asked one of them, "What are y'all doing?"

"We're Mayor Bloomberg's body guards," one of them said. "We're waiting for the signal to escort him in a parade."

The waitress delivered their breakfasts and the men started shoveling bacon, eggs, and toast into their mouths. Suddenly a two-way radio squawked and they stood up in unison. Before I could gather my wits to give any of them postcards, they grabbed their jackets and went out the door. I was getting that sinking, lost-opportunity feeling when one of the men hurried back in and headed for the men's room. He took care of that business, and on the way back through, he pulled bills out of his pocket and laid them on a table for the waitress. I had just enough time to grab a handful of postcards and thrust them into his hand as he rushed past our table on his way out.

"I hope you and the other guys will get a chance to go to this church sometime," I called out to his back.

God has His own way of letting us in on His work, and He has His own way of finishing it. Wouldn't it be great to see Mayor Bloomberg's bodyguards—and the mayor himself—in heaven?

***

Gregg, who was at that time pastor at Mosaic Manhattan Church (now known as Lower Manhattan Church) has since moved on to another church. When I followed up recently to ask what happened because of our mission trip, his email reply said, "We had many people come to church because they were handed a postcard. Passing out postcards rarely produced immediate fruit, but we always saw some. Thanks for your faithfulness! Gregg"

> *Sing a new song to the Lord! Let the whole earth sing to the Lord! Sing to the Lord; praise his name. Each day proclaim the good news that he saves.* (Psalm 96:1–2 NLT)

If you're willing, the Holy Spirit will give you boldness, too. And God will do all the work. New York City offered countless opportunities to be face to face with people—all day every day. In spite of its reputation for unfriendly or standoffish citizens, many of those folks wanted to talk about God. Write down three places where you are face to face with people in your own town: the grocery or drug store, a park, the bus stop, a shopping mall, your office lunchroom, etc.

_____

_____

_____

Chapter 6

God Goes Straight to Jail

Don and Susan visited our church for the first time about a year after we became members. When the pastor told the congregation to "Stand up and say hello to at least ten people around you," we saw them across the aisle and a few rows behind us. Wearing black leather vests covered with pins and patches, they stood out in the crowd. My husband, Chuck, wears brown cowboy boots and faded Levis with his shirt and tie, so he stands out among the suits and sport shirts, too. Anyway, we walked over to Don and Susan, said "Hello," and shook hands with them.

We could have left the worship service by any one of six doors, but on our way out that Sunday, we bumped into Don and Susan again. We struck up a conversation and quickly learned that they wore leathers because they rode a Harley Davidson motorcycle to church. The biggest patches and pins showed they were members of the Christian Motorcyclists Association (CMA). They explained that, among other ministries, CMA members regularly share the love of Jesus among the coarse characters at motorcycle rallies.

"We also go into prisons," Don said, almost as an afterthought. "They let us take our motorcycles right inside. After a speaker gives a testimony, the inmates huddle around us. Sometimes we're one-on-one. Or it might be a dozen at a time."

Chuck's face lit up. "I've been interested in doing prison ministry for years, but I don't have a motorcycle," he said.

"You're serious?" Don asked. Chuck nodded, so Don continued, "You won't believe this, but in just a few months Bill Glass Champions for Life—that's the prison ministry I was telling you about—is having a Weekend of Champions in the prisons right here in Austin. And you don't need a motorcycle to go."

"You could learn more at a fundraiser banquet this Thursday night." Susan added. "It's at the Holiday Inn near the airport. We're going. If you want to go, we can meet you there at six."

That Thursday evening we drove to a hotel, paid forty dollars each for dinner, and found seats at a table beside Don and Susan. At first that seemed a little pricy for a chicken dinner. But we would have paid much more, just to hear the speakers. And we learned that the ministry was worth it, too.

Mike Fletcher, a Christian former-champion-rodeo-cowboy-turned-comedian, warmed us up with hilarious jokes and stories about his life as a cowboy. Then ministry founder Bill Glass told the crowd how hungry incarcerated men and women are for hope, for love, and for the good news about Christ.

Bill Glass was a star defensive end for the Cleveland Browns football team and attended Southwest Seminary during his off-seasons. When he retired from football, Glass joined Billy Graham for a number of crusades. Then Graham and others badgered him about taking the gospel into the prisons. Frankly scared of the whole idea, in 1972 he said he would go "just one time." He took Roger Staubach and some other players with him and did a football clinic for the inmates, with miraculous results of inmate decisions for Christ.

Since then, Bill Glass and thousands of his Champions for Life volunteer "teammates" have been in thousands of prisons and jails. The teammates have learned to share their faith, and more than a million inmates have made decisions for Jesus.

It's all about His promise:

So if the Son sets you free, you are truly free. (John 8:36 NLT)

When we had lived in Colorado some years before, Chuck had experienced the joy of sharing Jesus with inmates as a volunteer chaplain's assistant. But I had no idea what prison ministry would be like. However, God was leading both of us to go. So, we registered for the Austin Weekend of Champions. A week later, a fat manila packet came in the mail.

Besides a welcome note, an information booklet, and some sample gospel tracts, the packet contained a list of "Do's and Don'ts." "Don't take in any knives and guns." "Don't talk during the programs!" "Don't run inside or outside a prison or jail." Obvious stuff. But we wouldn't have known not to wear all blue, all white, or all orange, not to wear open-toed shoes, or not to bring that "big thumper" Bible. Most of the do's made perfect sense: "Do relax." "Do mingle with the inmates." "Do be yourself." "Do listen twice as much as you talk."

> The apostle Paul wrote: *The good news is about his Son. In his earthly life he was born into King David's family line, and he was shown to be the Son of God when he was raised from the dead by the power of the Holy Spirit. He is Jesus Christ our Lord. Through Christ, God has given us the privilege and authority as apostles to tell Gentiles everywhere what God has done for them, so that they will believe and obey him, bringing glory to his name.* (Romans 1:3–5 NLT)

The time for the Weekend of Champions finally arrived. On a Thursday night in January, we went to that same Holiday Inn for a required training session. As we walked in the door, someone handed us a Champions for Life tract and copy of those "Do's and Don'ts." We sat near the front of a large ballroom full of chairs.

Our trainer was Jack Murphy, AKA "Murph the Surf." He was a long-ago entrepreneur in the surfboard industry, a concert violinist, an infamous jewel thief—and worse—who had been sentenced to double-life-plus-twenty years and should have been in prison until he died. But God had other plans.

Responding to visits from a steadfast chaplain and by Bill Glass and his team, Murph started his relationship with Jesus in prison and launched a prison ministry while he was still locked up. After his God-given early release from prison, he had become a ministry director for Champions for Life. If anyone could speak for the changes Jesus can make in a life, Murph could.

Murph called us and about a hundred other new Bill Glass teammates "freshmen" for our first expedition into the prisons and jails. He reinforced the do's and don'ts. He also explained that platform speakers would come into the units to talk to the inmates. He and other former criminals, as well as singers, strongmen, football, basketball, kickboxing, and baseball greats, all of whom had stories about a life-changing experience, would be "chumming the water" like a fisherman does, attracting many inmates who would never go to anything called "church." To give us an idea of what to expect, NBA halftime performer Tanya Crevier gave us a sample of her basketball juggling and spinning skills, any of which would put even the best basketball players to shame.

Then Jack gave us simple but thorough training on how to use the Champions for Life gospel tract, a reshaped version of ministry friend Bill Fay's questions and scriptures—the same Bill Fay who had come to our church in Colorado all those years ago.

"Look what it says on the front," Murph said. "It says 'What Do You Think?' Nobody ever asks inmates what they think about anything! It's 'CHOW TIME!' or 'MAIL CALL!' But you will be asking them what they think!"

Murph pointed out a few of the freshmen teammates to join him on the stage and said, "Pretend you're inmates." He asked the volunteers the questions on the front of the tract, and they gave answers an inmate might give, "I don't know," "I'm probably going to hell," or even "I'm sure I'm going to heaven."

"You're taking the inmates' spiritual temperature," Murph told us. Then he asked the "inmates" if they wanted to hear what the Bible says, and they nodded.

"Now, everyone, help me out here and read that first Bible verse out loud." They did. He asked each one to explain what the verse meant to them. One said, "I don't know." And Murph said, "Let's read it again." Finishing the verses, Murph told us to ask each inmate another series of questions that would culminate in a decision. We were to wait silently for answers. "If someone says 'No' to any of these questions," he continued, "ask 'Why?' and wait some more."

God's Word would do all the work.

When the training session was over, four hundred more Christians, all veterans of Bill Glass Weekends of Champions, joined us freshmen for "Spiritual Enrichment." Filling every seat in the large ballroom, we rattled the ceiling with praise songs then absorbed an impassioned message from Bill Glass.

After that, we were ready for breakout meetings. Someone shouted out the names of the prisons and jails. When we heard our assigned units, Chuck went one way, and I went another. Our coordinators called the roll and gave us tan packets filled with tracts, decision lists, and inmate Bible study guides. Then they told us about transportation and explained what to expect in the units for the next two days.

***

Joining the other Bill Glass teammates to visit the inmates in Austin was simple. We registered online. And we showed up for duty. As Christ-followers, all we needed were an obedient willingness to share His love and a photo I.D. And so we began our journeys into prisons and jails across America.

As we introduce lost people to Jesus, we also get to watch wayward Christians commit to a renewed walk with Him. Again and again, both kinds of inmates' countenances change—from listlessly guarded when we meet them to joyfully enthusiastic when we leave. The hopeless find hope as they accept new life in Jesus. And prodigal sons and daughters find assurance as they rededicate their lives to Jesus. And we have become bolder in sharing our faith.

More than forty Weekends of Champions later, we are still experiencing the boundless joy of watching God work in prisons and jails. The following stories reveal some of the ways God blesses us when we simply show up for service; then He works through us to reach inmates, some of the "least of these." The authorities may have caught these folks in their sins. But they look just like people you meet on the street every day. To God, they need Jesus, the same way we do.

> Jesus said: *Then the King will say to those on his right, "Come, you who are blessed by my Father, inherit the kingdom prepared for you from the creation of the world. For I was hungry, and you fed me. I was thirsty, and you gave me a drink. I was a stranger, and you invited me into your home. I was naked, and you gave me clothing. I was sick, and you cared for me. I was in prison, and you visited me." Then these righteous ones will reply, "Lord, when did we ever see you hungry and feed you? Or thirsty and give you something to drink? Or a stranger and show you hospitality? Or naked and give you clothing? When did we ever see you sick or in prison and visit you?" And the King will say, "I tell you the truth, when you did it to one of the least of these my brothers and sisters, you were doing it to me!"* (Matthew 25:34–40 NLT)

Really, it's not scary. As a Christ-follower, all you have to do is register and show up with your Bill Glass nametag and a photo I.D., prayed up and ready to obey God's lead. Will you go? _____ (If so, see the Bill Glass ministry contact information at the end of this book.)

That First Jail

We went to our first Bill Glass Weekend of Champions in January of 2005. Chuck went to a men's facility near Austin. I went to a women's facility in Lockhart.

After our Thursday evening training, spiritual enrichment, and breakout meeting, thirty other women and I joined our coordinator on a bus early Friday morning for the forty-five-minute ride to the jail. Clutching our small Bibles and tan packets of tracts, study guides, and decision lists, we stepped off the bus into glaring sunshine that was working hard to chase away the morning chill. We signed in, handed our driver's licenses to officers at the front door, and entered the lobby. Inside, we encountered an ominous pair of thick, metal sliding doors—some units call all of those security doors Sally ports; others reserve the title for outside gates—that would take us into the serious part of the complex. But it didn't even faze me when, one at a time, those heavy doors slammed shut behind us. The Holy Spirit took care of that.

Walking down a hallway and through another door, we found ourselves outside, on what they called the "yard." It was an acre of rock-hard dirt, some weeds, and perhaps a few blades of grass, surrounded by fifteen-foot chain-link fences with curled razor wire on top. About a hundred white plastic chairs stood in rows facing a low platform at the farthest corner of the yard. Inmates, dressed in white cotton pullover shirts with collars, white stretch-waist pants, and thin, quilted, olive-green jackets, already occupied many of the chairs. It struck me that, except for those uniforms, the inmates could have been the women I encounter at the grocery store or at church. Other inmates were coming out of another building, single file, hands clasped behind their backs. Uniformed officers stood on the edges of the gathering group.

I looked around and didn't see my prayer partner, Shirley, a veteran teammate who was there if I needed any help. But I noticed one of the men who had ridden a motorcycle into the yard—these men bring their bikes into the female units because women like Harleys, too. He was making his way down the rows of inmates, shaking each one's hand. Wearing fringed black leather chaps and jacket over his blue jeans and denim shirt, and a big smile on his face, he was making the ladies smile, too. I'm not sure how it happened, but I found myself following him, doing the same thing. It was fun!

That Friday morning, after Bill Glass spoke to the women, he asked if any of them would like to begin a relationship with Jesus. One woman near me raised her hand, and I walked over to her. She said her name was Kim.

Kim and I stood in the shadow of the razor wired fence and read the Bill Glass tract. Then she prayed with me to give her life to Jesus, finding the freedom only He can give! It bears repeating:

So if the Son sets you free, you are truly free. (John 8:36 NLT)

It was so simple, so easy, so thrilling to share that moment with her. Writing her name on my list, and checking the "salvation" box, I couldn't wait to do it again.

> *And the King will say, "I tell you the truth, when you did it to one of the least of these my brothers and sisters, you were doing it to me!"* (Matthew 25:40 NLT)

You may not think you are cut out for prison, hospital, or homeless shelter ministry, but you are underestimating the power of the Holy Spirit. If you do it to one of the least of these, you will also be doing it to Jesus. Will you take that first step of obedience? _____Will you let Him work in and through you? _____

Across the Prison Yard

In the course of a normal Bill Glass Weekend of Champions prison event, my husband Chuck would be sharing the gospel with dozens of inmates, often a dozen at a time. He would be leading many of those inmates to a first-time relationship with God, praying with them to trust Jesus as their Lord and Savior, praying with others to rededicate their lives to Christ. He would be writing long lists of names on his packet so a chaplain could follow-up with those who had made decisions. And he would be exhorting men to get on track with God.

On one particular February weekend, however, Chuck had stood out on the prison yard in the relentless freezing wind all day Friday and all day Saturday. He had enjoyed the platform speakers' powerful testimonies, and he had watched and prayed as other teammates huddled up with inmates to share the gospel tract. But he had talked to only a few men himself. At the end of the afternoon on Saturday, Chuck didn't have a single name on his packet.

When the officers ordered the confined men back to prison life, the Bill Glass teammates stood aside, and the inmates lined up to file back to their dorms. Chuck, who had been standing on the edge of the group, was half thinking, half praying, *"What a bum day this was. I didn't reach anyone at all. Lord, I'm sorry I disappointed you."*

The officers dismissed the inmates, and the lines of men in orange jumpsuits quickly covered the distance across the yard. They were almost to the door of the dormitory building when one of the men turned and waved at the Bill Glass teammates with both arms.

"Hey, Chuck!" he shouted. "If you don't think you changed someone's life this weekend, you did!" He paused for breath. Then he added, "It was me!"

Tears of joy blurred Chuck vision as he watched the inmates disappear into the building. God had worked—even when Chuck felt like he had done nothing. That's right, Chuck had done nothing but show up—and talk to a few inmates about God.

> *May your ways be known throughout the earth, your saving power among people everywhere. May the nations praise you, O God. Yes, may all the nations praise you.* (Psalm 67:2 NLT)

That's all it takes. You just have to show up. God will do all the work. Will you show up? _____ Why? Or why not?

_____

_____

She Knew Nothing about God

Crying as if she wouldn't see tomorrow, the woman, dressed in a white uniform with the word INMATE stenciled in big black letters across the back, stood beside the officer's counter in the corridor outside one of the women's pods (dormitories). I was just close enough to hear her stammer, "Can...Can...Can...I...Can I...talk to the chaplain?"

"You will have to request an appointment," the officer answered, handing her a sheet of paper. The inmate wrote for a minute and handed the paper back.

And that, as far as the officer was concerned, was that.

The inmate just stood there, shuddering with sobs. Feeling the Holy Spirit's quiet nudge, I stepped up to the counter and asked the officer, "Is it okay if I talk to her?"

"I don't see why not," the officer said.

For this Bill Glass Weekend of Champions, I was one of thirty-five teammates in the Henley State Jail, near Dayton, Texas. As is the norm, subject to some do's and don'ts, the teammates pretty much had the run of the place. So, this officer was just following the rules the jail authorities allowed for us.

One remarkable thing about the Bill Glass ministry is that we didn't have to stop our fellowship with the inmates when rain ended our program time on the exercise yard. We just followed them inside and would stay with them through lunch.

Maybe a notch below school cafeteria food—but usually edible—the food in jails can be breaded mystery meat and lumpy potatoes. It also can be thin slices of white bread, buried by grayish baloney, or coated with a tan liquid that looks like gravy but turns out to be peanut butter blended with jelly. We love eating with the inmates, but not because of that gourmet food. But, showing we are not "above all that," we cultivate deeper relationships with the inmates when we break bread with them.

Anyway, only God could have arranged for me to duck into the corridor at the same moment the conversation at the officer's counter started.

"Do you want to talk to me?" I asked the inmate, who still shook with sadness. She nodded. As we walked through the double doors into her pod, I put my hand on her shoulder. "I'm Carol," I said. "What's your name?"

"Angela," she sobbed, leaning into me.

We sat down at a stainless steel table. "My sister's husband is missing!" she blurted. "He's been gone for two days. We don't even know if he's dead."

I put my arm around her through another storm of tears. Then I said, "God knows."

She looked at me, blinking and sniffling.

"Do you believe in God," I asked.

"I don't know anything about Him," she answered.

"He loves you," I said.

Her blank expression told me she was having trouble processing this concept.

Not knowing where to begin, I babbled on about how God created the earth, the birds, the flowers, and the butterflies. That He created Adam and Eve so He could love them, and so they could love Him back. But they sinned.

"I feel sick," Angela said abruptly. "Do you mind if I go lie down?"

"Of course not," I said. "Can I pray for you?"

She nodded.

"Heavenly Father," I prayed, "please calm Angela. Let her feel your loving presence. Be with her sister and her husband. In Jesus' name, amen."

She walked around the half wall to the bunk area, climbed to the top rack, and wilted onto the blue, plastic-covered mattress.

Well that helped a lot, I said to myself, feeling like a world-class klutz.

After lunch, because of the rain, the other Bill Glass teammates and I went into the chapel for the afternoon Champions for Life programs. Soon the inmates filed in. I scanned the faces, searching for Angela, but not really expecting to see her. But, among the last ladies to come in, there she was, only a few feet away from me. Her face was still puffy from crying.

I waved at her, and she waved back, even smiled a little. "Can I get with you later?" I whispered.

She nodded.

The first speaker, Zack Reynolds, played his harmonica and sang about how bad it feels to be in chains to sin—inside or outside prison—and how good it feels to find God's freedom. Then Sandi Fatow told her story. She just wanted to "smoke a little and joke a little," but found herself doing drugs with gangsters and rock stars, giving up a son, and almost dying from an overdose. One of the trustees passed around rolls of skimpy toilet paper to dry noses and eyes as Sandi told the women how completely her life had changed when she put her total trust in Jesus.

"Raise your hand if you want to experience this change, too," she finished.

Angela's hand went up, and I went to her as the other teammates huddled up with other inmates. In the aisle behind Angela, an inmate who had not raised her hand was just standing there, looking confused.

"You want to hang out with us?" I asked. She nodded. So Angela, the other inmate (who said her name was Barbara), and I made a little circle.

"If you died today, would you go to heaven?" I asked. Neither was sure.

"Is it okay if we read some Bible verses together?" I asked. They nodded.

As we read the scriptures on the tract aloud, I asked them what each verse meant. Angela shrugged, but Barbara explained the scriptures in words I wish I could remember, much more clearly than anything I could have said. And Angela began to brighten with the understanding of God's good news.

After the last scripture, I asked them if they had ever invited Jesus into their lives.

"I haven't," Angela answered.

Because of our earlier conversation, I expected that response from Angela. But I'm sure my mouth fell open when Barbara said, "Neither have I."

So, praying the words after me, both women asked God for forgiveness, confessed that Jesus died for their personal sins and rose again, asked Him to be Lord of their lives, to fill them with the Holy Spirit, and to make them the women He wants them to be.

Only God could have put together our little circle of understanding and prayer. In spite of my perceived inadequacies for the task, I couldn't even mess it up.

Two lost souls found their way to heaven. God did all the work. I simply showed up and responded to His promptings.

> Paul wrote: *Each time He (Jesus) said, "My grace is all you need. My power works best in weakness." So now I am glad to boast about my weaknesses, so that the power of Christ can work through me.* (2 Corinthians 12:9 NLT)

Just show up. God can use you, too! Even if you think you're a klutz— and maybe you are a klutz. Also, don't assume that, just because someone like Barbara has a wonderful understanding of the scriptures, she has already given her life to Jesus.

Who will you ask about their spiritual beliefs this week?

_____

_____

God's Word Spoils Satan's Ambush

For the Houston, Texas, Weekend of Champions—paying a Bill Glass special rate that was a fraction of the usual fare—we stayed at the elegant Crown Plaza Hotel downtown. At the Thursday evening breakout meeting after training and spiritual enrichment, our coordinator told us the simple transportation plans for the next day. We would walk a few blocks from the hotel and ride Houston's Metrorail to the jail. "Get off at the end of the line," she said.

As usual, the veterans, who had participated in Bill Glass events before, paired up with first-time teammates, the freshmen. I was the veteran, and my freshman prayer partner was Ashley.

We met in the hotel lobby the next morning for the walk to the train. After a short prayer, we headed out the door. Ashley, who had straight, chin-length blonde hair, appeared to be the most innocent fifteen-year-old anybody could find. I knew she had to be older than that, because teammates must be at least eighteen to go into the jails. But that was my first impression.

On the way to the train, Ashley told me a little about herself. "I'm twenty-seven, and I have two kids," she began. "My husband took the day off from work to stay with my youngest son, Josh, or I couldn't be here. Josh has a serious illness, and with the help of some great doctors, God is healing him, but we have to watch him carefully."

I said something about being sorry about her son and glad she had such a caring husband.

"I found Jesus just a few years ago," she continued. "Before that, I was strung out on drugs, and I was into all sorts of other bad stuff."

So much for my first impression, I thought.

The train whooshed in, and we stepped on. At the last stop, we got off and walked another two blocks to the jail. About ninety women teammates soon filled the lobby of the ten-story, red brick building that stands on the edge of downtown Houston. After we gave an officer our driver's licenses, eight of us at a time boarded an elevator. Escorted by an officer and the chaplain, our coordinator was distributing the teammates among the inmates' pods on the various floors, two of us in each pod. Eventually, my group of eight walked down corridor and arrived at a set of sliding metal doors. One opened and we entered the small chamber; then the door rumbled shut behind us.

"We have pods A through D in here," the chaplain said. "The women in C are the _____." She used a mouthful of initials that didn't register with me. "Does anyone have any problems about going in C?"

I didn't know what the initials meant, but knowing that God was in charge, I didn't have any problems. My prayer partner Ashley didn't either, so she and I went into C Pod, and the second door opened and closed behind us.

As many as fifty inmates lived in each of the other pods. But because C Pod held the medical or psychological cases those initials stood for, we found only a dozen or so women inside.

Only five of the inmates were up and dressed in stiff, tan, scrubs-like uniforms. One of them was mopping the floor. Three were sitting at one of three stainless steel, picnic-style tables. Another was wiping off a table. Some of the others were listlessly climbing out of metal-frame bunk beds, and a few stayed curled up under green blankets on blue, plastic covered mattresses, oblivious to these two Bill Glass visitors. A toilet flushed behind a white, three-foot cinderblock wall at the end of the room, and I could hear the sound of a shower running.

I sat down with two inmates at one table, and Ashley gathered a group around her at another. A few others joined us as they finished dressing. After reading through the gospel tract with the women in my group, I found that they had already asked Jesus into their lives, but had really messed up. They all wanted to rededicate their lives to Christ, so I led them in a prayer to do so. Ashley and her ladies did about the same.

After the rededication prayers, we talked about God, about changes, about futures. And some of the women told their tough stories. One even told me she had killed her husband after he repeatedly beat her and the kids up. As Bill Glass teammates, we don't ask inmates why they're in jail, but if they want to share, it helps them. And it often helps inmates see each other in a different, perhaps more empathetic, light. Eventually, Ashley and I found ourselves leading Bible studies with the inmates at our tables, using the discipleship booklets from our Bill Glass packets.

Sometime later, another woman crawled out of her bunk. She was startlingly tall, with spiked blonde hair reinforcing that impression. As Ashley and I talked with the other women, she would stride up to a table and shout.

One time she put her face right up to mine and said, "What are you doing in here?"

"We're sharing God's love," I said. "What's your name?"

"Bonnie," she said. "What's yours?"

"I'm Carol," I told her.

"Well, Carol," she sneered, "I have a curse on me."

"Can we pray for you?" I offered.

"NO!" she shouted, stomping away to lie on her bunk with her back to us.

When the platform speakers came into C Pod to share songs and testimonies, Bonnie got up and sauntered across the room to pick up one of the payphones that lined one wall. Yelling into the receiver in the hollow room, she made sure she didn't hear anything the speakers said. I wasn't really paying attention to Bonnie's words, but because she never paused to listen, I figured she wasn't even on the phone. However, she did this for both programs on Friday.

On Saturday morning, before we spread out to the inmate pods, the teammates gathered in the chapel, which the jail had set aside for our breaks. A few inmate drawings hung on the white cinderblock walls. The only other furnishings were a bunch of plastic chairs and two tables holding coffee and snacks. The group fit in the room all right, but, even with pleas to "Use your indoor volume," the din of ninety excited voices overflowed the chapel and echoed all the way down the hall.

Over the commotion, I told our coordinator about Bonnie and asked if she would lead the women in a prayer for this troubled woman in C Pod. "That's fine," she said, "but you lead the prayer."

"Well, okay," I said. I hadn't prayed in front of such a large group before, but I trusted the Holy Spirit to help me. So, I whistled as loud as I could, producing the same effect in the noisy room as the mute button on your remote. Then I told the teammates about Bonnie. Agreeing that prayer was the only solution, they stood up and joined hands all across the room.

"Our heavenly Father," I began, "please touch Bonnie with your loving hand, bind Satan's power over her, and give us the Holy Spirit's guidance and wisdom as we talk to her about Jesus. In the holy and powerful name of Jesus we pray." Ninety voices said "Amen."

Then we headed back to the pods. Ashley and I sat down with the C Pod women to continue our Bible studies. Immersed in conversations with the ladies at my table, I didn't hear what was happening at the other table—until the celebration erupted.

Ashley filled in the details on our way back to the train. "I almost didn't come today," she began. "But I'm so glad I did!"

When Bonnie had walked up to Ashley's table for the fourth time that day, shouting, "I have a curse on me!" Ashley quietly asked, "Would you like to join us?"

"I guess," Bonnie growled, still standing menacingly beside the table.

Handing Bonnie the Champions for Life gospel tract, Ashley asked, "You want to read these scriptures with me?"

"Why not," Bonnie snarled.

"Read number one out loud," Ashley said.

"For God so loved the world that He gave His one and only Son (Jesus), that whoever believes in Him (Jesus) shall not perish but have ETERNAL LIFE," Bonnie read.

"What does that mean to you?" Ashley asked.

"Nothing," Bonnie answered.

"Let's read it again," Ashley said.

So Bonnie read that scripture again, and again, and again. And she read the next scripture again, and again, and again. Little by little, she began to tell Ashley what she understood about the scriptures. Then we heard the celebration.

Ashley had rushed to my table, with a beaming Bonnie and the other inmates from her table right behind her.

"Bonnie just accepted Jesus as her Lord and Savior!" Ashley announced.

We all clapped and cheered. Everyone hugged Bonnie.

God had used a young woman with a sick kid, who had been through some major stuff in her life, who was also young as a Christian and new to this prison ministry. But she wasn't afraid of Bonnie. And she wasn't afraid to share the good news about Jesus.

And through His powerful Word, God had changed the life of this woman who was cursed. And I mean that literally. After she prayed, Bonnie's voice and even her appearance changed, from rock hard to velvety soft.

A few weeks later, one of the other women in C Pod wrote to Ashley in care of the Champions for Life P.O. Box. Ashley emailed me to share the news. While Bonnie waited to get her own Bible from the chaplain, she was borrowing other inmates' Bibles so she could handwrite the scriptures and study them.

And that's how God works.

> Therefore, if anyone is in Christ, he is a new creation; old things have passed away; behold, all things have become new. (2 Corinthians 5:17 NKJV)

God can use you to change a life, too! A commercial for chocolate chip cookies says, "Warning, spontaneous joy may occur." That's nothing compared to the kind of joy you experience when—just because you show up ready to obey the Holy Spirit's lead—Jesus changes someone's life. In the scripture above, Paul is writing about "anyone." Even Bonnie.

But who will introduce them to Jesus? Will you? _____

Locked Down at Lexington

We arrived in Oklahoma City on a Thursday afternoon, ready to join the other teammates and the Bill Glass Champions for Life staff, coordinators, and speakers for a Weekend of Champions. It was our ninth event, but every prison weekend is different. And this one was no exception.

For the first time since we had been going to prison weekends, Chuck and I were going to the same unit, Lexington Correctional Institution, located about an hour south of Oklahoma City. Additionally, instead of climbing onto a big bus or van on a Friday morning, we would be driving our own car to the prison.

Don, who had flown to Oklahoma from Georgia to be the teammate coordinator for this unit, rode with us. It was nice to have the travel time in fellowship with him and to know a bit more about what to expect. As coordinator, he had visited the unit the day before, arranging for our event. He told us that this time the prison officials had the whole facility on long-term, lockdown status. At least they were letting the Bill Glass team come, and we knew we were bringing some very good news, which we knew would set a number of those inmates spiritually free, regardless of their other circumstances.

To reach almost thirteen hundred inmates on the men's side, Chuck and his fifteen male teammates were going to have to hustle. As the only woman going into the facility, I would be going alone to visit forty female inmates. I hoped to talk to each of them during the two days.

On our way into the unit Friday, a German shepherd service dog sniffed each of us for contraband. An officer opened the double doors to the women's pod, and I went in. I looked around and saw two floors of closed cell doors surrounding a high-ceilinged room with several metal tables—their empty dayroom.

As I made my way from door to door, talking and praying with one or two women inside each cell, the barrier presented by the doors produced an interesting paradox. Because the inmates and I had to stand right against the door to hear each other, we were much closer than you might normally stand to another person. We could see each other through a four-by-six-inch slit of glass. And because the double panes of that small window had a pocket of open space between them, I could even touch the inmates' hands as we prayed together. It was intensely intimate.

What a joy it was to talk about Jesus and pray with those women. Though some were sleeping when I peeked in their windows, and others didn't want to talk when I tapped on their doors, many of the women read the scriptures with me and prayed to dedicate or rededicate their lives to Jesus. Several women knew Him well and had already begun to repair broken relationships with Him.

One even sang for me. Through the locked door, her lovely voice carried the melody across the empty dayroom. The words told of the sadness of being caught sinning, then accused, convicted, and locked away from family, friends, and home. And they told of the joy of finding God's love and forgiveness through Jesus, of dedicating mind and heart to a new life of obedience, and of seizing the chance to break the chains of sin. The last note echoed across the room. Then, with tears in our eyes and our fingertips just touching in the space between the glass panes, we prayed as two Christian sisters.

***

I felt a joyful peace when I joined Chuck and the other Bill Glass teammates for lunch.

Because the inmates remained locked in their cells, we wouldn't be eating with them, a fellowship time we usually enjoy. Instead, we went to the officers' dining room for lunch.

After lunch, we were just waiting around. We asked our coordinator, Don, what was taking so long. He said we had to wait while inmate trustees delivered food trays to all those cells, and while the officers did their customary count. Since it seemed like an endless stretch of downtime, Chuck and I asked Don if we could spend it visiting any inaccessible inmates. Because we had spent time with Don on the way to the jail, he knew our hearts and our experience in prisons. He didn't mind, and the officers didn't mind.

Inaccessible often means the high-security area, or even death row, but this time it was the prison's medical center. We found ourselves with some inmates who were in another lockdown situation. Though they weren't in locked cells, they were in what amounted to a hospice.

I suppose I knew that, besides the death-row inmates, the life-sentence inmates—and those who contracted terminal diseases—would eventually die in prison. But it had never occurred to me how or where they would die. Those lifers, and other inmates who couldn't go home or who couldn't afford care in an outside medical facility, wouldn't ever be going anywhere else.

We separated to talk to as many of those inmates as we could. As I walked across the room, Chuck sat down beside a man who was almost as white as the sheet and blanket that covered him. The man looked about as sad as a person could be.

I heard Chuck introduce himself and ask the first question, "Why are you so sad?"

Because I immediately focused on another inmate, I didn't hear the rest, but Chuck told me later.

"I have cancer all over my body, and I'm going to die soon," the man said. "I'm afraid I'm going to hell."

Chuck held the man's hand and, using the Champions for Life gospel tract, read him scriptures where God promises heaven to those who believe in a risen Christ, and who have accepted His full payment for their own sin debt.

"I prayed to invite Christ into my life years ago," the man said. "Even though I messed up and ended up in prison, I still believe. And I'm following Him as best I can."

They talked some more. Finally, understanding God's promises for prodigal sons, the inmate cried tears of relief as Chuck said a prayer of assurance with him. Then Chuck reminded him of God's promise:

> *So now there is no condemnation for those who belong to Christ Jesus. And because you belong to him, the power of the life-giving Spirit has freed you from the power of sin that leads to death.* (Romans 8:1–2 NLT)

***

I had crossed to the other side of the room and sat down beside a Hispanic man, who was propped up in bed with a white sheet and blanket tucked around his shoulders.

"I'm Carol," I said. "What's your name?"

"I'm Jorge," he answered. "I'll be going home soon."

I said that would be nice. Then, not knowing how long we might have to talk before our coordinator came to get us after the count, I asked Jorge straight out if he thought he would be going to heaven one day. He said he wasn't sure. I read him the gospel scriptures in the tract, and we talked about each one. Then I asked Jorge if he had ever accepted the gift of God's forgiveness that's only available in Christ.

"No, I haven't," he said.

"Would you like to pray to receive that gift right now?" I asked.

He nodded and put his chin against his chest to pray. Repeating the words with me, he invited Christ into his life, asking for the forgiveness Jesus died to offer.

As soon as he said "Amen," he started thanking me. "Thank God instead," I told him. "It was all God's plan and all God's work."

Later, I learned from an orderly that, when Jorge said he was going home, he wasn't going to make it back to his earthly home. Since he had just committed his life to Jesus, however, I knew Jorge would be going home to be with Jesus, whenever the time came.

***

While I was talking with Jorge, Chuck had moved along to visit a patient behind another closed door. This time the door was a barrier to the tuberculosis inside. Knowing that God wanted him to share the love of Jesus, Chuck donned a mask and surgical gown and went inside. The man listened to the gospel message and said he needed to think about it. On the bunk in his small cell, he had nothing to do but think. Now he had something new to think about, and he had the gospel tract Chuck left with him.

***

I told Jorge I needed to move on and talk to some other men. He readily agreed, so I went into another room, where I found a man lying in a recliner on wheels. Watching a high-perched TV, the man probably weighed over five hundred pounds.

"Hi," I said. "I'm Carol. Can I hang out with you for a while?"

"Sure," he said. "I'm Andy."

Still not knowing how long we would have before our coordinator came for us, I got right to the point.

"Do you believe in God?" I asked.

"I guess so," he answered.

"Do you believe in heaven and hell?"

"Well, yes."

"Where would you go if you died today?"

He wasn't sure, so I asked if he wanted to hear the Bible verses that would explain how he could be sure he was going to heaven.

"Yes," he said, "I would really like to know."

He didn't move, and one of his eyes stayed shut as I read the scriptures to him and we talked about what each of the verses meant. But he started to smile, beginning to understand how much God loves him. Then Andy and I prayed together. He confessed his trust in Jesus alone for salvation and invited Him into his heart and life. Big tears rolled down the side of his head from his good eye, dropping on the vinyl of the recliner just behind his ear.

Not more than a minute later, Chuck came into the room. I introduced him to Andy. Though he still hadn't changed his position on the recliner, Andy was beaming. I think he would have been dancing around the room, if he could have.

"Your wife is such a wonderful person," he said. "I can't believe she just brought me such good news."

"Well, here's the thing," Chuck answered. "We just show up, and God does all the work."

"Well, thank you," said Andy, "for showing up."

***

Lunch and the count in the jail continued, so God had given us more time in the medical unit. Looking around, I noticed that three inmate orderlies, who had been working with the patients, were finally taking a break. They said they had seen Andy's joyful response from across the room. I asked if they would like to hear the good news I had shared with him, and they sat right down on a bench to listen. We went through the scriptures in the tract, and the inmates told me what each verse meant to them. At the end, all three of those young orderlies prayed to invite Jesus into their lives!

We had just said "Amen" when Don arrived to take us back to the general population inmates for the rest of the afternoon.

***

On Saturday, we spent the morning talking and praying door-to-door with the general population inmates. After lunch, we again asked if we could spend the downtime in the medical unit. The officers and Don said "okay."

When Chuck and I returned to the clinic, the three inmate orderlies still glowed with the newfound joy of salvation. They wanted to learn how to tell somebody else this great news!

So I taught them how to share the Champions for Life tract with other inmates and their families and friends. I also talked to them about daily prayer, Bible time, going to chapel services, and finding a good church when they got out.

While I was doing that, Chuck went back to talk with the dying cancer patient. He told me the man—who had been so completely hopeless the day before—was smiling.

"So, how are you doing?" Chuck asked.

"I'm going to heaven!" the man said.

***

Then Chuck joined me in the hallway of the medical unit. Through a fishbowl of windows, we could see maybe twenty inmates sitting in rows of chairs in another room. We asked an officer if we could talk with them. "No, these men are new to this unit," she said. "They're waiting to be processed through medical. We can't allow you to talk to them."

Though it seemed to us that they would have been the best candidates for the changes offered by our risen Lord, we didn't argue. All we could do was hope the new and old Christians who had just prayed with our teammates would pass the good news along to them—even through the walls of their locked cells.

I nodded toward several other inmates sitting on benches in a nearby hallway. "How about those men," I asked, "can we talk with them?"

"Yes," the officer said. "They're just waiting for medical appointments."

Walking over to the inmates, I asked, "Is it okay if we hang out with you for a while?"

"We don't have anything else to do," one said with a laugh.

That's how seven more men, waiting on that bench for medical appointments, heard the gospel message. And six of them prayed to receive the forgiveness and love of Jesus. The seventh man stared across the room while they prayed. But he had heard the truth, and it's up to God to finish His work with him.

As those men left to talk to doctors, three others replaced them in the hallway. Two sat down on the bench beside us. One of them, a twenty-something black man, who said his name was Lee, had come for his own appointment. The other, David, a white man in his early thirties, had brought the third inmate—an older man named Jack, who remained in a wheelchair beside him—to see the doctor.

We asked about their spiritual beliefs. Jack was sure he was going to heaven and gave a Christ-centered reason; the other two had no idea.

As Chuck shared the gospel message, Lee leaned forward, devouring every word. David slouched against the wall. When Chuck asked Lee and David if they were ready to commit their lives to Jesus, Lee was eager to invite Jesus into his life.

"I'm not ready," David said. "I have my doubts. But it's interesting that you would be here today," he added, nodding toward the man in the wheelchair. "I just got Jack here as my "cellie" yesterday. We already started this conversation [about Jesus] a couple of hours ago. Then he got called for this doctor's appointment, and I had to push him over here."

David asked question after question, and raised doubt after doubt. With words only the Holy Spirit could have inspired, Chuck answered each question thoughtfully, and Jack backed up Chuck's answers with scriptures he quoted from memory. Eventually an officer shouted out Jack's name, and he wheeled himself away to see the doctor.

Jack was gone for a solid thirty minutes. This gave David—who would have been locked in a cell, and perhaps not interested in talking to one of our teammates through a door—a whole block of time to hear more answers to his questions and doubts. After this miraculous amount of uninterrupted time, Chuck asked David again, "Are you ready to commit your life to Jesus?"

"I don't want to do it in jail," he said. "Everybody has a prison conversion. It never sticks."

"So," Chuck said, "you're like everybody?"

David didn't say anything.

The officials had somehow allowed the other inmate, Lee, to sit on the bench all that time, too. He patiently listened to David's questions, Chuck's answers, and Jack's scriptures. All of that seemed to intensify his determination to make Jesus Lord of his own life.

When Chuck asked Lee if he still wanted to pray with him, he answered, "Definitely!"

Chuck prayed the prayer on the tract, with Lee repeating each phrase. After they said, "Amen," Chuck began to tell him how to start his walk with the Lord: daily prayer and scripture reading, going to church, and telling others about Jesus.

I turned to David. "Can I tell you about a woman in another jail who told me she wasn't ready to commit to Jesus either?" I asked.

He nodded.

"She said, 'I just can't soften my heart.'"

This manly man—who found himself in jail, at the lowest point of his life but not ready to commit to Jesus—turned to look at the wall, but I could see a tear making its way down his cheek.

As David composed himself, Jack rolled up in his wheelchair, ready to return to their cell. And our coordinator came to take us back to the inmates behind the locked doors in the pods. And that's our Lord's timing!

We left David to God's care, and to the Bible wisdom of his cellie. We won't know this side of heaven whether David was able to soften his heart and let Jesus in. That's God's job. We just show up to do our part, pray, and leave the rest to Him.

> So God's rest is there for people to enter, but those who first heard this good news failed to enter because they disobeyed God. So God set another time for entering his rest, and that time is today. God announced this through David much later in the words already quoted: "Today when you hear his voice, don't harden your hearts." (Hebrews 4:6–7 NLT)

The above scripture about hard hearts quotes a man named David. As for the inmate David, I'm praying that he doesn't wait too long to soften his. Don't worry about how you will share the good news, or how others will receive it. God will take care of everything. All you have to do is show up. Will you show up? _____ Why? _____

From Prison to Pastor Times Two

Chuck and I drove from Austin to Perry, Georgia, arriving on a Thursday afternoon and checking in at the Holiday Inn, where the Bill Glass Champions for Life staff, speakers, and teammates were assembling for a Weekend of Champions. Following directions to an old church on the other side of town, we joined hundreds of other Christians who had come from churches in Georgia and all across the United States. We arrived in time for freshman training (required for first-time teammates and optional for any others who, like us, appreciate a refresher). Again, our trainer was Jack Murphy, the former jewel thief—an extreme example of a life changed by Jesus—who entertained and trained us, by role-play and exhortation.

Afterwards, the veteran teammates joined us, filling every seat in the sanctuary and spilling over into the choir loft. We shook that old church with praise and worship. Then Bill Glass gave an inspiring message about sharing the love and hope found in Jesus, the only One Who changes lives.

After Bill's closing prayer, Tully Blanchard—a former World Champion wrestler God had also led to the ministry's leadership team—called out teammate jail and prison assignments. When he shouted Houston (pronounced "house ton") County Detention Center, Chuck and I stood up and followed our coordinator, Howard, to a corner of the room for a breakout meeting.

You guessed it. Chuck and I were going to be in jail together again.

That weekend, of the teammates assigned to this detention center, the women outnumbered the men almost three to one. And of the inmates, the males outnumbered the females three to one. Since I had been on many Weekends of Champions, Howard asked if I would go with Chuck to the men's side.

As we entered the facility the next morning, it crossed my mind that I might be self-conscious on the men's side, especially with Chuck in the pod with me. But as the second door of the Sally port clanged shut behind us, the Holy Spirit filled me with the same peace I always have in the women's units.

I walked over to a few of the men in orange jumpsuits who sat on backless stainless steel stools attached to stainless steel tables—nothing comfortable in jail—in the pod's dayroom. Others came out of some of the surrounding cells to find out what we were doing there. I was telling them we had come to share God's love with them when our platform speakers came in.

Some of the inmates had planned to sit out the programs in their six-by-ten-foot cells. But when they saw through the glass slits in their cell doors that one of the platform speakers was Jenn Harris, a female with long, blonde hair, most of them came out and leaned against the railing upstairs. Some of them slipped down the metal steps to stand around the edges of the dayroom downstairs.

Jenn played a guitar and sang some bluesy songs. Then she told what God had done through some excruciating ordeals in her life. Tully Blanchard shared vivid details of his life—before and after Jesus came in. They left the inmates with an invitation to learn more about Jesus by talking with one of us teammates. Several more men in orange uniforms soon huddled around the table where I was sitting. As we went through the gospel tract, the men read the scriptures aloud and shared thoughts about what each verse meant.

Disregarding what the others in the pod might be thinking, the huddle of men prayed with me to dedicate or rededicate their lives to Christ. What an honor! God allowed me to watch as He touched those men with the good news that Christ died to pay for their sins—and they could be forgiven!

***

There's more to the story.

Saturday afternoon, after the speakers had gone, I approached a table where three inmates were playing dominos. "Do you mind if I sit with you?" I asked. They motioned to an empty stool.

"What did you think about the speakers?" I asked. They all liked them. I asked if they had gone through the tract with anyone.

Two of the men said they had. They were Christians and had rededicated their lives to Christ. Though neither of the two said much more, I knew I would remember Joe. I'm only five feet tall, and this black man barely came up to my shoulder. Besides being different in stature, I remember Joe because he just didn't look like somebody who would ever spend time in jail. He had a certain radiance about him.

I had quite a discussion with the third man at the domino table. A tenacious non-believer, he asked questions, listened to my answers, and hammered me with still more questions. Though the Holy Spirit gave me more good answers than I thought I had in my head, and we didn't argue, the inmate wouldn't budge in his resistance to God's love. I won't know until I get to heaven what God did with him afterwards. However, Joe and the other inmate had also heard our discussion. I prayed that what we said had reinforced their faith.

Around three-thirty that afternoon, as Howard came into our pod and was trying to shepherd us toward the Sally port to leave, Joe tugged at my arm, saying, "I'm getting out of here next Wednesday! Would you pray for me?"

"Of course," I said, "what would you like me to pray about?"

"For my strength when I get out and that I would follow God," he said.

We moved a few feet away from the others and I prayed for him.

"I would like to write to you," he said. "And I want to go into jail with your ministry one day."

I wrote my name above the Champions for Life address on a tract. "You're welcome to write me at this address," I said. "I'll write you—if you write me first. When you've been out, off paper, and clean for a year, contact the ministry about going back into the jails with us. Lots of former inmates who succeed with Jesus in their lives go back into prisons and jails to rescue somebody else."

***

Many inmates say they will write me, but very few actually do. Joe was different. The courts released him as scheduled, and he wrote me several letters over the next few months, thanking me for the profound impression I had on his life.

I don't remember all the Holy Spirit gave me to say to the men huddled around the tables that weekend—even the answers I gave the persistent non-believer. And the brief prayer with Joe had happened on my way out the door. Obviously, it had been God's influence on him, not mine.

In his last letter, Joe wrote, "Carol, I now have my minister license, and look forward to a distinguished theological education. None of this would have been possible without your help at Houston County Detention Center early this year."

It took my breath away. Again, I had no idea that anything the Holy Spirit led me to say in that jail would have such an impact on this man's life. All I did was give my life to serve God. Then I simply showed up. And God did all the work.

> Now all glory to God, who is able, through his mighty power at work within us, to accomplish infinitely more than we might ask or think. Glory to him in the church and in Christ Jesus through all generations forever and ever! Amen. (Ephesians 3:20–21 NLT)

It really doesn't take any special talent to share the love of Jesus. You simply obey the Holy Spirit. He will tell you what to do and say. Will you obey?_____

***

Another inmate in the men's unit of the Houston County jail that same weekend stands out in my mind. Unlike Joe, this black man named Russell towered over me.

It was Saturday morning. Chuck and I were hanging out with the men in the pod's dayroom before the Bill Glass speakers arrived. Russell was one of the men gathered around a table, no doubt curious about what this short, gray-haired lady was doing in their pod. "What has God been doing in your lives," I asked them.

"He's turned my life completely around!" Russell said. "About three years ago, when I was in the free, I found a new life with Jesus. I found a new wife, and I even accepted a position as pastor of a small church. Then I came to jail for this thing I did before I found Jesus. You know," he said, looking straight into my eyes, "the day I turned myself in was the best thing that could happen to me."

"How's that?" I asked.

"Well for one," he began, "I will not have that mistake hanging over me. I'm paying my penalty for what I did. Two," he continued, "I have lots of time on my hands here in jail, time to focus on reading and studying the Bible. I have time to think, without the distractions of stuff that goes on in the free. And three," he went on with a wide grin, "God is already using me right here in this jail." Then he added, "And guess what. That church still wants me to be their pastor when I get out!"

> Jesus said: *We must quickly carry out the tasks assigned us by the one who sent us. The night is coming, and then no one can work.* (John 9:4 NLT)

God can use you, too—right where you are. How is He using you?

_____

_____

_____

_____

_____

The Officer and the Inmate

Holding our breath, we didn't see how our seventy-something-year-old driver would squeeze the big shiny bus through the narrow gateway and into the parking lot of Indiana State Women's Prison—which stands in an old part of Indianapolis—without knocking some bricks off the eight-foot wall or bending a corner of the bus. But somehow, with much turning, backing, and adjusting, he finally did it.

Exhaling almost in unison, the fifty Bill Glass Weekend of Champions teammates on the bus gave the driver a standing ovation. Volunteers all, we piled down the steps of the bus, quickly checking nametags and organizing ourselves into alphabetical order outside the razor-wired fence. We shivered in the early-morning chill as we signed our names on a list, handed an officer our driver's licenses, and entered the prison. The iron gate banged shut behind us.

Inside the walls, we found bluegrass edged with flowers surrounding red brick buildings. The place looked more like a college campus than my preconceived notion of a prison. Bright sunshine was beginning to warm a large open space, where more than two hundred folding chairs already formed rows across the grass. We scattered ourselves out among the chairs as inmates in white uniforms started appearing from their dormitories.

Not knowing what to expect from this rag-tag bunch of strangers who had come into the prison that Friday morning, the inmates wore expressionless faces. We greeted them with smiles and handshakes, and saw those faces start to reflect our smiles as the women filed along the rows of chairs and sat down.

Our platform speakers were Tamra Comstock, who belted out some blues songs, and Tanya Crevier, who juggled, bounced, and twirled a bunch of basketballs, asking inmates to help her, showing the smallest one how to hold a spinning basketball on her fingertip. The women responded with energetic clapping and cheers.

Tamra and Tanya told the inmates their own stories of the forgiveness and life changes that had happened since they met Jesus. Tears ran down many faces as the inmates began to grasp a glimmer of hope that this could actually happen to them, too.

After she gathered up the last of ten basketballs she had been spinning in her finale, Tanya asked the inmates to huddle around us teammates to find out how they could make their own first move toward that change.

At our meeting the night before, the veteran teammates had paired up with freshman prayer partners who had never been on a Weekend of Champions. That morning in the prison, my two prayer partners were sitting among the inmates in the row behind me. They looked at me expectantly as six inmates turned to us for that life-changing information from God's Word. I'm sure my teammates wanted me to lead the whole group while they watched.

Instead, I said, "Those are yours," and nodded toward the inmates on their row. "Just like they showed us last night at freshman training, have them read the verses with you, and ask them what they think." No longer hesitating, they gathered the four women around them, and I turned to the two beside me.

After we read and discussed the scriptures, my two inmates wanted to restore their broken relationships with God and prayed to rededicate their lives to Jesus. I was thrilled, as I always am when someone feels God's tug on a heart and, like the prodigal son, makes that U-turn back to Him.

I was also thrilled that evening when the whole Bill Glass team gathered at a church for barbeque and celebration. With tears of joy, one of my prayer partners stood up and told everyone how she had shared the gospel tract with the four inmates. All of them had prayed with her to make Jesus their Lord and Savior. "Until today…" Her voice cracked and she stopped. Then she began again, "Until today, I had not shared the good news about Jesus with anybody. Now I know the joy I was missing. I can't wait to do it again!"

**

And God was still at work the next day. After the morning programs and sharing time on that Saturday, when the inmates went back to their dorms for a head count, the teammates gathered in the chapel for a bathroom break and snack. The chaplain and the prison superintendent spoke to us briefly, thanking us for coming. I figured my prayer partners were ready to continue sharing the tract with inmates, so I asked the superintendent if I could talk to the women in the lockdown unit. Those women would not be coming to the Bill Glass programs—or anything else for a while.

"I'll discuss it with the chaplain and get back to you," he said.

The first speaker of the afternoon program, strongman Paul Wren—get this—drove a nail through a two-by-four with his hand protected only by a folded handkerchief. Then he allowed the biggest officer (a man who probably weighed more than two hundred fifty pounds) to jump from a table onto his stomach. No worse for those experiences, he had grabbed the inmates' attention. In a gruff but tender voice, Paul told them about the differences knowing Jesus made in his life.

Ex-drug addict Sandi Fatow was to speak next. It was getting late and I began to think the chaplain must have forgotten about the lockdown women. But as Sandi was adjusting the microphone, our coordinator told me that the superintendent and chaplain had given me and one other teammate permission to visit those women. She said I could pick the other teammate.

God had already given me the teammate, a black woman I had noticed on the bus and during breaks. I didn't know her, but her face and actions simply radiated the love of Jesus. As I expected, she was excited about going into the lockdown unit with me.

An officer escorted us to one of the red brick buildings, unlocking heavy doors, and banging them shut as she left us. We found ourselves inside a dreary hallway. As our eyes adjusted, we saw an officer sitting at a desk in the middle. Cells with iron bars lined both sides. One woman occupied each cell. Starting in opposite directions, we went from door to door, talking to the hurting women, telling them how much God loves them, inviting them to come to Jesus, or to return to Him.

The four women I encountered had many hurts to share, and we discussed the scriptures on the gospel tract at length. Two prayed to ask Jesus to take over their lives for the first time, and two rededicated their lives to Him. Real changes were in store for them, right where they were in that lockdown unit. My teammate was making her way down the other side, talking and praying with the others. We were the perfect team, as God always provides.

When I looked up after praying with the last of the four inmates, I saw that my teammate was talking to the woman behind the last door on her side. The only other lockdown inmate was sitting beside the officer's desk in the middle of the hallway, carefully folding a stack of trash bags.

"Did you already talk to the other lady?" I asked the inmate, nodding toward my teammate, who was following an officer back outside to the courtyard.

"No," she answered.

"Would it be okay if I talk to her?" I asked the officer, whose nameplate said Ms. Bradford.

"That's fine," she answered.

The young woman was a tiny mouse of a person. She hardly seemed the type you would expect to find in a lockdown unit, where inmates often find themselves segregated because of what officers and inmates alike call "knuckleheaded"—often violent—behavior.

Stifling my curiosity about why she was in jail, and why lockdown, I asked, "Why are you folding those trash bags?"

"I'm not sure," she answered flatly, "but it gets me out of the tank for an hour."

Then I asked her name. "It's Shyra," she answered. *That suits her perfectly*, I mused.

I asked Shyra if she believed in God, and I asked if she believed in heaven and hell. She said, "Yes," to both questions. When I asked where she thought she would go if she died that day, she said softly, "I don't know."

"Would it be okay if we see what the Bible says?" I asked, handing her a gospel tract.

Again, she simply said, "Yes."

When I asked her to read the first scripture aloud, she said, "I can't."

The Holy Spirit nudged me with a wild idea, *"What about the officer?"*

Of course, I reasoned, *she's sitting right there.* So I asked, "Officer Bradford, would you help us read the scriptures?" And she agreed!

So, Officer Bradford read the scriptures, and I asked both women what each verse meant. Shyra didn't have any idea. But as she read the verses—several of them more than once for Shyra—the officer gave simple, accurate explanations.

When we finished talking about the last scripture, I asked each of them, "Are you a sinner?" Each woman nodded. "Do you understand that Jesus died to pay for your sins and that He rose again?" They nodded again. "Have you ever accepted His payment for your own sins and made Him your Lord and Savior?" Neither of them had.

Given their respective positions in the prison, and the fact that we were in the hallway, I wasn't sure how they would respond to the next question.

"Would you like to pray with me to accept that gift now?" I asked.

They both said yes! It was something I couldn't have imagined in my craziest moment of optimism. But God could.

So, holding hands with me in the middle of the lockdown unit, not caring what anyone else thought, Shyra and Officer Bradford prayed to accept God's gift of eternal life through Jesus.

Of course, God had worked it all out long before I showed up.

> *When His disciples heard it, they were greatly astonished, saying, "Who then can be saved?" But Jesus looked at them and said to them, "With men this is impossible, but with God all things are possible."* (Matthew 19:26 NKJV)

Seeing what God does, in you and through you, is the most fun you'll ever have. Will you join us? Will you tell someone about Jesus? _____

What about that Afro?

Silently praising God, but not doing cartwheels—partly because I was in a prison and partly because I probably would have hurt myself—I left the lockdown unit of Indiana State Women's Prison. Inside those doors, He had touched several lives, including an officer and an inmate *at the same time*, with the miracle of denying self and embracing Jesus.

Another officer escorted me back outside. Blinking in the sunshine, I saw that the inmates were beginning to disperse to their dormitories after the last program of the Bill Glass Weekend of Champions. The other teammates and I would be getting back on our big silver bus soon.

Walking along the sidewalk toward the teammates and inmates, who still lingered on the lawn in scattered groups, I encountered Sophia, an inmate I had briefly spoken with the day before.

The timing had to be God's work. In a matter of seconds, Sophia would have been back in her dorm. Only seconds earlier, I was still inside the lockdown unit. But here she was, walking toward me.

***

Though I had arrived in Indianapolis just two days before, this divine appointment had actually started a few weeks before, with Destiny, a fifteen-year-old girl I was mentoring at a juvenile detention center in San Marcos,

Texas. During our first Tuesday-night meeting, she had prayed with me to ask Jesus to take over her life.

After that momentous night, my visits with this extremely bright black girl had alternated between laughing or crying about the "drama" in her dorm and talking about her future and her relationship with God. One Tuesday evening, she met me with a big grin on her face. However, her smile wasn't the most striking thing about Destiny that night. She was completely bald!

"What in the world happened to your hair?" I asked.

"I'm trying to grow a 'fro'," she said. "You know, an Afro."

I knew about Afros, all right. But I hadn't seen anyone wearing that cotton-top look since the late sixties and early seventies.

"Who did this to you?" I asked.

"My DI [drill instructor] did it," she answered, still grinning with her whole face. "You have to shave your head to get it started right."

I had to take her word for it. After all, I didn't know anything about starting an Afro? *But,* I said to myself, *what was that drill instructor thinking?*

"Well, you're beautiful—with or without your hair," I said. That was our last Tuesday visit before she was released, so I don't know how Destiny's Afro turned out. But God was going to use it to change the life of an inmate in Indiana.

***

In the Indiana prison the day before, I had sat right behind a young woman whose hair surrounded her head like a soft, black cotton ball. It was a picture-perfect 'fro.'

What a great way to start a conversation, I thought. *The program won't be starting for a few minutes. I'll find out if my mentee was messing with me.*

I tapped the inmate on the shoulder, and she turned around in her chair. "Your hair is great," I said.

"Thanks," she replied.

"Here's the thing," I said. "The kid I mentor at a juvenile center back in Texas was totally bald when I went to see her last month. She says you have to shave your head to get an Afro started right. Was she messing with me, or did you shave your head, too?"

"Yes, I did," she answered. We both laughed.

I asked her name. "It's Sophia," she said.

I was saying, "I'm Carol," when the coordinator tapped the microphone to introduce the first Bill Glass platform guest. Later, when the inmates gathered around us after the program, Sophia wasn't in my group. And I lost track of her.

But, as I left the lockdown unit that Saturday afternoon, there she was, walking with her friend toward their dormitory. Because I had been so interested in her hair the day before, I recognized her face. This time, however, her hair was not fluffy. It was flat against her head.

I stopped her. "Your hair still looks great, but what happened? Did you cut it?"

"No, I waxed it," she said, giggling with her friend.

Knowing that the Bill Glass teammates would be leaving soon, I didn't waste any time. "Did you discuss this with anyone?" I asked, holding up the folded gospel tract.

"Yes," she said.

That wasn't enough for me. "Did you pray with anyone?" I asked. She shook her head no.

"Can we talk about it some more?" I asked.

"Sure, I guess so," she said.

Sophia's friend's name was Sara. And with a joyful smile that showed it, Sara said she had already talked about the tract with another teammate and had prayed to receive Christ that morning. But she wanted to hear the scriptures again, too. So the three of us went back to the folding chairs and sat down.

We read the scriptures together, and I asked them what God's Word was saying. I could see by Sophia's expressions and answers that she was gaining a clear understanding that God loved her and wanted a personal relationship with her, which is only available through Jesus. I explained that the relationship started with her decision to accept His payment for her sins. "No one else can make the decision for you," I added, "not your friend, not your family, not a preacher or church."

"So, according to the Bible, are you a sinner?" I asked, reminding her that we had just talked about the scripture that says, "All have sinned."

She said, "Yes, I am."

Then I asked, "Would you like forgiveness for your sins?"

"Yes," she said.

"Would you like to pray with me to ask Jesus to forgive your sins, come into your life, and change you forever?" I asked.

With tears rolling down her cheeks, Sophia said, "Yes, I would."

Praying each phrase after me, she asked God for forgiveness. Saying she believed Jesus died to pay for her sins and that He rose again, she made Him Lord of her life, and committed her life to Him.

Again, I was ecstatic. God's perfect work and His perfect timing had allowed a meeting that was almost missed, a fleeting moment. He had been planning this forever, lovingly arranging all the details. This love—a love that sent His Son to pay the ultimate price for our sins—invites everyone to love Him back.

> *Even before he made the world, God loved us and chose us in Christ to be holy and without fault in his eyes. God decided in advance to adopt us into his own family by bringing us to himself through Jesus Christ. This is what he wanted to do, and it gave him great pleasure.* (Ephesians 1:4–5 NLT)

> *But God demonstrates His own love toward us, in that while we were still sinners, Christ died for us.* (Romans 5:8 NKJV)

Your approach can't fail. After all, it's God's message, not your eloquence. And God will arrange even the smallest details. Are you ready to share the story of God's love with someone? _____

The Officer on Tour

During the daily count time, and between programs at a Bill Glass Weekend of Champions at a women's prison in Gatesville, Texas, two corrections officers took our group of teammate volunteers on a tour of the areas where the inmates worked. A female officer led the group, talking about sewing and cabinetmaking programs as we walked.

A male officer and I brought up the rear. I saw that he was simply acting as an escort, sort of a babysitter for us. So, as we followed the group between the buildings, I asked him, "What do you think it takes for a person to go to heaven?"

He considered the question for maybe a minute. "Well, I've mostly been a good person," he answered.

"Would you like to hear how the Bible answers that question," I asked.

"That's fine," he answered.

While the female officer showed the rest of the group the inmate work areas, the male officer and I stood against the farthest wall. It was awkward to be reading the tract. So, I quietly shared the F.A.I.T.H. outline and verses I had committed to memory. He heard the scriptures that tell us that we are sinners in need of forgiveness for our sins, that God's forgiveness is available but not automatic, that it's impossible for God to allow our sin into heaven. The officer's face lit up with understanding as I explained that when we turn from our sins and turn to Jesus, accept His full payment for our sins on the cross, and ask Him for forgiveness, He will give us an abundant life here and eternal life with God—heaven.

The officer wasn't at all embarrassed to stand on the edge of the group and pray with me. Repeating the words of a simple prayer, he admitted that he was a sinner in need of a Savior, that Jesus died on the cross to pay for his sins and rose again, and he invited Jesus to come into his life and make him the person God wants him to be.

We finished our prayer just as the tour ended, witnesses to another display of God's impeccable timing.

> God be merciful to us and bless us, and cause His face to shine upon us, that Your way may be known on earth, Your salvation among all nations. (Psalm 67:1–2 NLT)

God will arrange the timing for you, too. Will you try Him out? _____

Why Was Johnny Hesitating?

It was a warm fall night. Chuck and I had spent an hour with our mentee kids in the gym at the juvenile detention boot camp near San Marcos, Texas. We were walking across the parking lot to our car.

"I wonder if those people need some help," Chuck said.

This was odd. Chuck never notices these things. I do. If I see a man, he says, "He knows what he's doing." If it's a woman, Chuck changes the tire, or whatever.

This time was different. I hadn't even noticed the man standing by the dark Chevrolet Camaro with the trunk open, but if I had, I probably would have heard my internal warning system say, *Get in the car and lock the doors*. After all, we were in the parking lot of a detention center. Anyone who wasn't a uniformed officer or a mentor would have to be one of those dreadful family members our mentees often told us about.

But Chuck headed toward the dark car, saying, "I'm going to see if I can help."

I was hurrying to our car, planning to get in and lock the doors, when I heard Chuck say, "We'll give you a ride to that Shell station up the road."

The man was probably just as nervous about getting in the car with us at the detention center as I was about him. I heard him say, "Wait in the car, honey, I'll be back in a few minutes."

I hadn't noticed the man's wife either. He no doubt thought she would be better off taking her chances in the parking lot.

Anyway, that was how this thirty-something man named Johnny, who was indeed the father of one of those juveniles, ended up in the back seat of our car. "They ran out of gas," Chuck said to me. "We're taking him up to that Shell station."

We chatted a little about what a pain it is to run out of gas. It wasn't long before I asked Johnny my favorite question, "If you died today, would you go to heaven?"

He didn't answer right away. It crossed my mind that it was crossing his mind that we might be planning to help him get there sooner.

"No. I'd probably go to hell," he finally said.

"Why is that?" Chuck asked.

"I've done lots of bad stuff," Johnny replied.

"Would you like to hear how the Bible says you could be sure you would go to heaven instead?" I asked. "It won't take long."

"Sure!" he said.

As far as my seatbelt would allow, I turned in my seat to look at Johnny in the back seat behind Chuck and shared the F.A.I.T.H. scriptures, which were handy in my head—memorized. As we drove up beside the pump at the gas station, Johnny's expression was saying that he was thrilled with the idea that

God would forgive his sins, so I asked if he wanted to pray to invite Jesus into his life.

But Johnny said nothing.

He and Chuck got out of the car to pump gasoline into a red plastic container. I sat in the front seat, wondering why he didn't answer.

By the time Chuck and Johnny got back in the car, I was about to burst.

"Why are you hesitating to ask Jesus into your life?" I asked.

"I want you to tell my wife first," Johnny said.

I loved that answer.

Back at the detention center parking lot, we found his wife still sitting in the passenger seat of their car. She was talking on her cell phone.

"Hang up, Mary! You have to hear this!" Johnny shouted through the open car window.

She shrugged in annoyance that she should be in such a big hurry to hang up, but she said, "I gotta go. Bye," and got out of the car.

We stood beside their car, and Chuck repeated the scriptures to both of them.

Johnny paced up and down like a caged tiger.

Chuck finally finished the last scripture. Then he asked each of them, "Would you like to pray to ask for God's gift of forgiveness through Jesus?"

Mary nodded, and Johnny grabbed her hand and Chuck's. We stood in a little circle under the lights of the detention center, and they prayed after Chuck, "Heavenly Father, I know I'm a sinner. Please forgive me. I believe Jesus died for my sins, and that He rose again. Jesus, I make you Lord of my life. Please change me and make me the person You want me to be. Thank you, Lord Jesus. Amen."

As soon as he said "Amen," Johnny began to bounce around the parking lot like a kid on a pogo stick, his face barely containing his grin.

God had taken any fear we had of each other and turned it into His glorious moment. All we had to do was be ready to listen for the still, small voice of the Holy Spirit and immediately obey His instructions. For all of Johnny's celebration, just think of the celebration that went on in heaven that night.

In the same way, there is more joy in heaven over one lost sinner who repents and returns to God than over ninety-nine others who are righteous and haven't strayed away! (Luke 15:7 NLT)

Has the Holy Spirit been talking to you? _____ Will you speak out boldly and watch Him work?_____

If you're inspired to join the teammates for a Bill Glass Champions for Life day or weekend, see Resources and Contact Information at the end of this book. Register for an event on the Website. Then write down the names of five Christian friends you will invite to visit "the least of these" with you. Keep in mind that you may have to invite them five times before they go.

_____

_____

_____

_____

_____

Chapter 7

God Sends a Blizzard of Tracts

Our pastor, Michael Lewis, regularly invited outside evangelists to speak at our church. Those speakers encouraged any unsaved members of the congregation to make Jesus the Lord of their lives. They also urged those of us who had already received the gift of salvation to tell others about Jesus.

One Sunday night, Pastor Lewis introduced our speaker, saying, "This is Glenn Chappelear. He's a professional fisherman."

"A professional fisherman?" Chuck whispered. God doesn't worry about unusual combinations, however. He makes all of us fishers of men.

> *Jesus said to them, "Follow Me, and I will make you become fishers of men." They immediately left their nets and followed Him.* (Mark 1:17–18 NKJV)

Right away, Glenn proved how well he could fish by wrapping a line, sinker, and hook around a volunteer's ear from twenty feet—without spilling a drop of blood.

Having caught our full attention, too, he told us about his ministry. As he travels to fishing competitions, people at gas stations and hotels ask about his state-of-the-art fishing boat. This often gives him the opportunity to introduce them to Jesus. When the situation isn't right for a long conversation, he hands the person a gospel tract. "Researchers have found," he explained, "that at least one out of every ten people who read a gospel tract will accept

Jesus as Lord and Savior. I have no idea which one it will be, so I pass out lots of tracts." His salvation stories included one about a tract someone plucked out of a trashcan, and another about a tract that was stuck in gum on someone's shoe.

At the end of Glenn's message, Pastor Lewis climbed the steps to the stage and showed us the "Thank You" tracts he gives to restaurant servers with his tips. "You will find these in the new plastic bins around the church," he told us. "We print these on our own printer, so they are just pennies apiece." He offered one caveat: "Don't leave one on the table unless you also leave a nice tip!"

After the worship service, Chuck and I headed straight for one of the bins and grabbed a handful of the folded quarter sheets. We read "Thank You" on the front, gospel scriptures and a salvation prayer inside, and the church address on the back. We began to pass out the Thank You tracts to everyone we encountered, grabbing more every Sunday. Eventually, it occurred to us that the Thank You tracts were great for restaurant employees, grocery store cashiers, and even the person who held a door open for us. But they weren't quite right for the person behind us in the checkout line or beside us at a gas pump.

Since I'm a writer, I decided to put together a tract myself, one we could give to anyone. As you can see by the sample that follows, one side of the quarter-page tract says "Good News! You are Invited to Go to Heaven!" And it asks "If you died today, would YOU go to heaven?" Inside, scriptures explain the gospel message, followed by a salvation prayer. The back encourages readers who have just made Jesus Lord of their lives to tell someone—a pastor if possible. It also recommends praying and reading the Bible daily, as well as another important practice: attending a Bible-based church. It includes our church address and phone number.

We pass these "You are Invited" tracts out as God increases our territory. Besides our everyday travels around Austin, we regularly travel to deliver my husband's artwork to galleries, and we travel to share the good news about Jesus with inmates in prisons across the country.

Saying, "This is for you," or "I would like to share this with you," or "Here's something to read when you get a break," we give tracts to folks at gas stations, grocery stores, motels, and galleries. We have slipped them into purses, baby strollers, car windows, truck beds, and telephone booths. We leave them with our tips for the housekeepers at Super 8 Motels. Trips from Austin to Dallas to take care of my aging mother for two weeks at a time for three years further increased my territory. I encountered more people at doctor's offices, physical therapy sessions, new grocery and drug stores, and a procession of people who came to do maintenance work on Mother's old house.

Although it's not always easy to hand out tracts—I sometimes get shy—it usually is simple. At least 95 percent of the people simply take the little paper and say "Thank you." Some decline, saying, "I'm already a Christian." When that happens, I say, "Would you give it to somebody you meet for me?" I often add, "Make sure you're going to heaven. And take as many people with you as you can."

A few people say they just don't want it, but honestly, I have passed out thousands of tracts, and only two of those folks have yelled at me. No doubt, some tracts end up in trashcans. But I also believe that God has used some of the tracts somebody discarded in ways I can't even guess.

The following stories tell about some people who gladly received the tracts—and some who resisted. We won't know, this side of heaven, how God worked in the lives of all the people who ended up with those little slips of paper. Or even what He did with those rare individuals who said "NO!"

> Then He said to them, "The harvest truly is great, but the laborers are few; therefore pray the Lord of the harvest to send out laborers into His harvest." (Luke 10:2 NKJV)

Are you ready to join in the harvest? _____ **Why, or why not?**

_____

_____

_____

_____

_____

The gospel tract we use appears on the following pages:

Note: This is a mock up of the tract. Permission to make reprints granted if you will be distributing them free of charge. Print four on a page, double-sided, cut in quarters, and fold in half. For the MSWord document, email cwrite4jesus@aol.com.

Do you know for sure where you will be in 100 years?
Heaven or hell? It's your choice.
Consider what the Bible says:

1. *"The heavens declare the glory of God."* (Psalm 19:1 NKJV) God created the universe, and He created you. He wants a loving relationship with you. But your sin separates you from Him. *"For **all** have sinned and fall short of the glory of God."* (Romans 3:23 NKJV)

2. The result of your sin <u>should</u> be spiritual death (hell), but God gave you a way out, a gift. *"For the wages of sin is death, but the **gift** of God is eternal life in Christ Jesus."* (Romans 6:23 NKJV)

3. God loves you. *"But God demonstrates His own <u>love</u> toward us, in that while we were still sinners, Christ died for us."* (Romans 5:8 NKJV)

4. That gift is eternal life with God because of His forgiveness through Jesus. *"For God so <u>loved</u> the world that He gave His only begotten Son, that <u>whoever believes in Him</u> should not perish but have everlasting life."* (John 3:16 NKJV)

5. Jesus said: *"I am the way, the truth, and the life. <u>No one</u> comes to the Father <u>except through Me</u>."* (John 14:6 NKJV) So, <u>only faith alone in Christ alone can save you</u>.

6. *"Christ died for our sins, according to the Scriptures, and that He was buried, and that He rose again on the third day, according to the Scriptures."* (1 Cor. 15:3b–4 NKJV) <u>After</u> the crucifixion, Jesus appeared to the disciples and to five-hundred others before He went to heaven.

7. Jesus made a specific promise: *"He who hears My word and believes in Him Who sent Me has everlasting life and shall not come into judgment, but has passed from death into life."* (John 5:24 NKJV)

8. But Jesus also said: *"Unless you repent, you will all likewise perish."* (Luke 13:3 NKJV) Repentance is changing your mind to recognize who Jesus is and being sorry enough about your sins to let Him change you as you accept His authority and follow Him.

9. It's your choice. *"If you confess with your mouth the Lord Jesus and believe in your heart that God has raised Him from the dead, YOU WILL BE SAVED!"* (Romans 10:9 NKJV) YOU can take this step of FAITH by saying something like this to God:

    My God and Heavenly Father, I am a sinner, and I know I deserve hell. I am sorry I sinned against you. I'm turning away from my sins and turning to Jesus. I believe Jesus died to pay the penalty for ALL MY SINS, and rose from the grave. I trust Jesus alone, and not my works, for my salvation, and I make Him Lord of my life. Thank you God for the forgiveness and everlasting life I now have. Since I will need a lot of help to have the relationship You desire with me, please empower me with Your Holy Spirit, and make me the person YOU want me to be. Amen.

10. From now on, your good works will <u>prove you are His</u>. *"For by grace you have been saved through faith, and that not of yourselves; it is the gift of God, not of works, lest anyone should boast. For we are His workmanship, created in Christ Jesus for good works, which God prepared beforehand that we should walk in them."* (Ephesians 2:8–10 NKJV)

¿uǝʌɐǝɥ oʇ oƃ noʎ plnoʍ 'ʎɐpoʇ pǝᴉp noʎ ɟI

¡uǝʌɐǝH oꞱ o⅁ oꞱ

You Are Invited

¡sʍǝN poo⅁

- - - - - - - - - - - - - -

Fold Here

If you have read the message inside, and you just prayed this prayer and meant it, God has forgiven your sins, and you are on your way to heaven. You are ready and able to do those good works God has prepared for you because you are now a new person. *"If anyone is in Christ, he* [or she] *is a new creation; old things have passed away; behold, all things become new."* 2 Cor. 5:17 (NKJV)

What do you do now? Your next step of FAITH is to tell someone. 1) Call or stop into a Bible-based church and tell the pastor. Ask him about baptism. 2) Read your Bible daily (begin in John (the fourth book of the New Testament); then read the next two books, Acts and Romans and the rest of the New Testament; and then read the Old Testament), 3) Pray (talk to God) every day, and 4) Now that you are forever related TO God, attend a Bible-based church to grow in your new relationship WITH Him.

We would love to hear from you. Please call, email, or visit us:

Your Church Name, Physical Address,
Email Address, and Phone Number Here

© Carol Middlekauff 2013

Tattoo Girl

Chuck and I were traveling west across Mississippi toward home in Austin, Texas, after a Bill Glass Weekend of Champions ministry in some Georgia prisons. Just after dark, we stopped for the obligatory gasoline and potty stop.

While Chuck pumped the gas outside, I headed for the "hers" inside.

Passing the magazine rack, I couldn't help but notice a couple browsing there. The twenty-something woman wore a black tank top and shorts. Harsh tattoos covered almost every other inch of her, from the jet-black hair, which stood in three-inch spikes on her head, to the tops of her bulky black boots. She had piercings everywhere. The young man with her was just as threatening. Their overall demeanor flashed anger and defiance like a neon sign. My steer-clear-of-them reflex kicked in.

Though it was in His usual small voice, I clearly heard the Holy Spirit say, *"Give her a tract."*

Instead of handing the girl a tract, however, I slipped down an aisle on the farthest edge of the store. Pushing open the door to the ladies' room and latching the cubicle door, I was negotiating with the Holy Spirit: *I'll give it to her if she's still there when I come out.*

I took my time washing and drying my hands. Business done, I thought, *Surely they'll be gone by now. Nobody spends that much time in a convenience store.*

I was wrong. I walked out of the ladies' room and past the cashier, and there they were, browsing through the chips.

That was it. I had to give her the tract.

With the small slip of folded paper in my hand, I walked up to her.

"This is for you," I said.

Her hands were full of snacks, so I stuck it between her fingers and a Big Gulp cup, fully expecting her to drop it before she made it back to the car.

I was wrong again.

The pair paid for their snacks and walked outside. I hung out in the candy aisle, heaving a big sigh of relief and waiting for Chuck to come out of the men's room.

Suddenly the man burst back into the store!

I didn't even have time to be terrified.

Within an arm's length of the staring huddle of customers waiting to pay for their junk food, he shouted in my face, "Why did you give that *thing* to my wife?"

"God told me to," I said. Even to me it sounded crazy. But it was the truth.

"Well, it offended her!" he barked.

"I'm sorry," I mumbled. He turned and stomped out the door.

I guess the part about being sorry wasn't quite true. I wasn't sorry. I know God works in mysterious ways, and He had told me to give the tract to that young woman. I also know that when people are struggling with Him, they can become extremely sensitive to His Word, reacting fiercely to its conviction.

Shaking from head to toe, I said to myself, *I planted a seed, or maybe I watered it, and I won't know this side of heaven what will happen next.* Then I prayed that this tattooed person will find her way to (or back to) God—and her husband, too. I have a feeling it will be the answer to the prayers of someone else in her life, who must be praying just as intensely as she is resisting.

> *It's not important who does the planting, or who does the watering. What's important is that God makes the seed grow. The one who plants and the one who waters work together with the same purpose. And both will be rewarded for their own hard work.* (1 Corinthians 3:7–8 NLT)

Epilogue: We drove on down the highway, my mind involuntarily sorting through a list of bad stuff that might happen in the darkness. It didn't. However, I've regretted one thing: I missed the opportunity to give tracts to the cashier and all those people in line. I have no doubt that God will send someone else for them. I only know that I clearly heard His call to give the tract to the tattoo girl.

> *It is the same with my word. I send it out, and it always produces fruit. It will accomplish all I want it to, and it will prosper everywhere I send it.* (Isaiah 55:11 NLT)

I once heard someone say that tracts are like tickets to heaven. How many people will be traveling with you? _____ Will you put some tracts in your pockets? _____ And will you give those tickets away? _____

The Walgreens Harvest

I was at Walgreens, stuck in a long line to order a prescription. As I often do, I said hello to the woman behind me and handed her a tract. Though she appeared to be in her forties, she was leaning on a walker.

"What's this?" she asked.

"It tells you how to get to heaven," I answered.

"That's great," she said cheerfully. "But I'll have to find someone to read it to me."

"Do you need it in Spanish?" I asked, digging in my purse for a Spanish tract.

"No, I just need help reading it," she replied.

As we both put in orders for medicine and stepped aside to wait for the pharmacist to fill them, my mind clicked away: *I wonder if she can't read. Or maybe she can't see. Surely she has a friend who can read it to her.*

The Holy Spirit had other ideas. *"You read it to her,"* He nudged.

Of course, I said to myself. *I can read it to her. We're both here for the duration.*

"Would it be okay if I read it to you?" I asked aloud.

She smiled and nodded.

We moved a few feet away from the others, and I read the scriptures on the tract, asking what each verse meant to her.

Within a few minutes, right there in the Walgreen's aisle between the Ace Bandages and Tums, she was praying to invite Jesus into her life.

This time, the memorized F.A.I.T.H. outline wasn't even necessary. I just read her the tract, asked her what the scriptures meant to her, and let God's Word touch her heart.

God had blessed me with the privilege of watching the birth of another baby Christian. As we talked about how her new life should begin with Bible study, prayer, and church, I invited her to our church.

"I think the lady I work for goes to that church," she said. "What a small world!"

A small world, indeed, when God sets up the meetings.

> Jesus said: *You know the saying, "Four months between planting and harvest."*
> *But I say, wake up and look around. The fields are already ripe for harvest.*

The harvesters are paid good wages, and the fruit they harvest is people brought to eternal life. What joy awaits both the planter and the harvester alike! (John 4:35–36 NLT)

It's as simple as reading a tract with someone. Look around you. You'll find plenty of people who need some good news, who will let you share that joy. Where can you find those people in your world?

_____

_____

_____

Those "Chance" Encounters

Chuck and I were driving home to Austin from a Bill Glass Weekend of Champions ministry in a juvenile detention facility in Tecumseh, Oklahoma.

Almost to Hillsboro, about sixty miles south of Dallas on Interstate 35, our car dinged out an alarm to tell us it needed gas. I thought we should go on to Waco because the gas prices are always at least a nickel cheaper. Chuck didn't want to risk driving another forty plus miles past Hillsboro when the car was already asking for gas.

"We never know how far that last little bit will go," he said, "and somehow I don't think you would fancy walking five miles to save a nickel a gallon."

Passing the first exit, Chuck steered off the freeway at the second Hillsboro exit. Then he drove past Shell and Exxon stations right beside the exit ramp, crossed the bridge over the Interstate, and rolled up to an island at the Love's Truck Stop.

Chuck got out to pump the gas, saying he was also going inside to use the restroom. At first, I didn't unfasten my seatbelt, thinking, *I really don't need to go. We'll be home in a couple of hours.*

But I felt a nudge from the Holy Spirit, *"Go in and give out a few tracts."*

Tucking three gospel tracts in the back pocket of my jeans, I headed inside.

I handed the first one to the man who held the front door open for me on his way out of the store. As I went into the ladies' room, I gave one to a woman who also was on her way out. Inside, I handed the last one to a young woman who was drying her hands. I don't know what God did with the first two tracts. But what happened with the third one answered one of my prayers.

As I went into the stall, the woman asked through the partition, "Are you from Austin?" She must have been reading the back of the tract, which included our church's address.

"Yes," I said, pushing down on the flush handle and waiting for the noise to subside. "I'm Carol."

"I'm Melissa," she said, as I came out and washed my hands. "I'm from Killeen. I'm on my way home from the NASCAR races at Texas Speedway."

Barely pausing for breath, she gushed on about this incredible driver, Kyle Busch, who had won the day's race from a position way back in the starting lineup. He had been driving for the company she worked for, but he had recently joined the Joe Gibbs racing team. I supposed that could have made him some sort of a traitor to her, but she was mostly impressed with his driving.

"Was Kyle Busch driving the Interstate Batteries, number eighteen car?" I asked.

"Yes," she answered. "How did you know?"

"This is too much," I said. "Just a few hours ago I was at a juvenile detention facility with a Bill Glass prison ministry, and one of the speakers, Jack Meeks, brought a retired Interstate Batteries #18 car right into the unit. After he blasted our ears revving up the car's motor and smoking its tires across the courtyard, he told the kids it had won the Daytona 500 in 1993, and that Kyle Busch was the new driver for the current #18. Then Jack told the kids about his own early life of crime and what changed after he turned his life over to Jesus."

"Thank you," she said.

"What for?" I asked, wondering what I had said.

"I got out of prison three years ago," she answered. "I found Jesus because someone like you visited me while I was locked up."

So, God had set things up so I would be in the ladies' room with this particular person.

"As you can see," she continued, "I'm still out. And just as He promises, since Jesus took over my life, I'm a brand new woman. I'm a brand new wife for my husband and a brand new mom for my children!"

"God is great!" I said, hugging her. "And it's my turn to thank you, Melissa. You are my first live evidence—besides the speakers and teammates who come with us on Bill Glass Weekends of Champions—that turning to Jesus really changes inmates. And that they stay changed after we leave. After they get out."

"Well He does! And I did!" she said.

I practically danced my way back to our car, praising God for giving me another special appointment, for showing me how He changes people. We always see big changes in inmates' countenances while we're inside those walls, as their expressions go from hopeless or skeptical to glowing with joy. But now God had given me a random someone outside the curled barbwire, whose life Jesus had changed forever. And, of course, if Jesus changes just one life forever because I tell lots of folks about Him, it's all worth it.

> *Still other seed fell on fertile soil. This seed grew and produced a crop that was a hundred times as much as had been planted!* (Luke 8:15 NLT)

If you share the love of Jesus, He will change the lives of people you touch, too—and the people they know. Who have you shared with lately? Or who will you share with this week?

_____

_____

Shocked at the Bus Stop

Driving down an Austin street, minding his own business, Chuck passed two men sitting on the bench at a bus stop. They weren't just any two men. They were dressed in black, with spikes everywhere a person could wear them and piercings and chains everywhere else. One even had spiked hair, and the other had shaved his head, except a two-inch section in the middle—a Mohawk. Those looks weren't in style that year, and it wasn't Halloween.

For Chuck, it was one of those can't-get-out-of-here-fast-enough moments. Thinking, *If they aren't crazy, they're probably mean,* he kept his foot on the accelerator. However, for God, it was an opportunity. The Holy Spirit said, *"Go back and give them tracts."*

Chuck's first response was, *You've got to be kidding. Those guys don't want to hear about Jesus. Besides that, they're not anywhere near my age. Please send somebody else.*

However, he made a U-turn at the next wide spot in the street and went back, hoping the bus would hurry up and come.

It didn't.

Getting out of the car and approaching the two men, Chuck figured they couldn't have been much out of high school. He pulled two tracts out of his shirt pocket.

"I'd like to share these with you," he said, more than half expecting the young men to use their big black boots to kick the lunch out of him. As they took the tracts, Chuck was planning which way he might run before they could do it.

That wasn't how it went.

The guys said, "Thanks," and started reading the folded slips of paper. Chuck decided not to run just yet. This might be good.

They read awhile, and then looked at each other and at Chuck. "This is weird," one of them said, gesturing with the tract. "We just watched a DVD of *The Passion of the Christ* last night. We weren't sure what to make of it, but this answers a lot of questions."

"That movie really hit me," the other man said. "And beside that, I just turned thirty-three, the same as Jesus. And my initials are J.C."

Before Chuck could reply, the bus rumbled up the street, screeched to a stop, and opened its doors. The guys climbed aboard, saying, "Thanks a lot!"

Chuck walked back to the car, amazed. All he had done was reluctantly obey the Holy Spirit's urging, when it didn't make any sense to him at the time. Once again, God had reminded him that He loves everyone—no matter what we might think of them.

> *For God so loved the world* [even the people we think are scary] *that He gave His only begotten Son, that whoever believes in Him should not perish but have everlasting life.* (John 3:16 NKJV)

Don't let your judgment of someone keep you from doing God's work. Name some of your fears and prejudices, and pray right now that God will help you set them aside.

A Father, a Son, and Angels

Driving from Austin to an artist's reception at the Booth Western Art Museum in Cartersville, Georgia, Chuck and I were still pinching ourselves and praising God that thirty-one of his paintings would be a featured in this wonderful museum. They called his exhibition "Route 66 Meets Highway 41: Roadside Impressions by Chuck Middlekauff." Chuck had been painting cowboys and Western Americana for seventeen years, and selling lots of his work in galleries, but we had thought museum shows were strictly for famous artists—or dead ones.

Nevertheless, we were on our way to Georgia for Chuck's oral history interview, artist's reception, and a PowerPoint presentation in the museum's auditorium. It was definitely a God thing.

We stopped at a Louisiana convenience store to fill our car with gas and use the restrooms. Though we weren't too low on fuel, and we weren't quite desperate to use the bathroom, we just stopped. Chuck got out to pump the gas. Following my usual pit stop procedure, I grabbed a handful of tracts for the people I would encounter and headed for the ladies' room.

On my way, I passed a car parked near the door. Through the open car window, I could see two men. Barely slowing down, I handed the man on the driver's side two tracts, saying, "These are for y'all."

I went inside and took care of my business. On the way out, I passed Chuck on his way in. Then I passed the two men. They were no longer sitting in their car.

One of them stopped me, saying. "Could we talk to you?"

"Sure," I said, trusting God.

My eyes fastened on the younger man, who was sitting on a low yellow railing, smoking a cigarette. His shoulder-length, curly brown hair, brown eyes, and dazzling smile made me think, *If I were going to paint a portrait of Jesus, I would use this guy as a model.*

The other man, who had gray hair and mustache, was across from him, leaning against the hood of their car and waving a tract at me.

"I'm Doug," he said. "And this is my son Blaine. We have been driving from Mississippi to Houston, but Blaine has this bad habit and needed some smokes, so we stopped. You won't believe it, but when you handed us these, we were sitting in the car talking about angels."

Chuck joined us, catching the end of Doug's comment. We all shared some thoughts about angels: that the Bible tells us that they are not sexual beings, that, as mighty warriors, they fight a constant battle with evil around us, and when they have come to earth for certain special occasions, they appeared as males. It also says we might find ourselves entertaining one.

Then Chuck changed the subject. "If you died today, would you go to heaven?"

"Yes, of course," Doug answered.

"Umm, I'm not really sure," was Blaine's reply.

"Why would God let you in heaven?" Chuck asked, looking at Doug.

"Because Jesus Christ is my Lord and Savior," Doug said.

"Why aren't you sure?" I asked Blaine.

His father answered for him. "Of course he's sure. He went forward in church and got baptized when he was twelve."

"That's great," Chuck said, looking at Blaine. "So, why would God let you in heaven? Or why wouldn't He?"

"I don't know…," Blaine's voice trailed off. Then he began again, "I've just had some doubts lately. I don't think He will let me in with doubts."

Pressed for specific doubts, Blaine said, "I'm seeing the evil in the world, wondering where God is in all of this. Why do such bad things happen to people? And why do people do such bad things?"

Explaining that God doesn't cause evil, but people do evil through the influences of Satan, Chuck assured him that everyone has some doubts or questions sometimes.

Doug mentioned some of the Bible heroes who had expressed doubts, questioning their own abilities, and even questioning God's presence of mind in considering them to do His work. "But God used them anyway. Look at Moses, Abraham, Mary, and Peter," he said.

"People have prophesied over Blaine," Doug added. "He's only seventeen, but they have said he will be a preacher, a pastor, one of God's messengers."

"We're not angels or prophets," Chuck said to Blaine, "but we do know that God uses us, in spite of our weaknesses—and maybe because of them. He can use you, too, even if you have doubts."

"We all have our times of doubt," Doug added, "and that's where faith comes in."

"I wish I had someone I could talk to about these thoughts," Blaine said, "someone I could trust."

"It's always good to have a Godly man to talk to," I said. "And it looks like your dad is one of them." Blaine smiled and nodded at his dad.

"I haven't been the father I wanted to be," said Doug, "but I'm going to start."

We offered Blaine more words of assurance and encouragement, saying that Jesus doesn't desert us when, like the prodigal son, we wander away from Him. He just waits for our return. We assured Blaine that only his acceptance of God's gift of eternal life through what Jesus did on the cross and His resurrection will give him acceptance in heaven, not how he feels on a certain day.

Blaine began to express his confidence and trust in Jesus, and as the conversation wound down, we offered to pray for Blaine and Doug. They grabbed our hands and bowed their heads.

So, outside the door of a convenience store, on our way through Louisiana toward an improbable art exhibit in Georgia, we prayed with Doug and Blaine, who were headed the opposite direction. Paying no attention to the people walking by us, we asked God to help this young man spend the rest of his life following Jesus, open the lines of communication with his dad, and find God's purpose for his life.

It was all God's work, a divine appointment that started with a couple of little tracts. The end of the story remains in His hands.

> *Night and day we pray earnestly for you, asking God to let us see you again to fill the gaps in your faith.* (1 Thessalonians 3:10 NLT)

Be honest with yourself. What's keeping *you* from doing God's work?

_____

_____

_____

Chapter 8

Running God's Race

In the Bible, Paul plainly tells Christians they are running a race, the race God sets before them. It's a spiritual race.

I run physically, too. A few years ago, depending on what I was training for, on a given Saturday I might have run three to ten miles on the wide, hilly trail around Lady Bird Lake. I had been doing it since Chuck and I moved to Austin.

After committing my life to God's fulltime service, I began to sense that I wasn't using His time fruitfully. As I ran on the trail Saturday after Saturday, year after year, I was getting fitter. But suddenly, running mile after mile, often hour after hour, seemed like a waste of His time.

Because I had memorized the gospel scriptures and LifeWay's F.A.I.T.H. outline, I knew I could share the good news with anyone—anytime. One morning I was praying about this, and God gave me an idea: I would wear a race tag pinned to the back of my running shirt. The tag would say "JOHN 3:16" on the first line, and "WORLD = YOU" on the second.

I typed those lines in a big, bold font, and I added Great Hills Baptist Church and its Website in smaller letters below. I printed it out on a half sheet of paper, and Chuck (the artist, who has the hand skills in the family) attached it to one of my old running tags that's made of paper that won't tear no matter what. Then he sealed it with clear packing tape. Practically indestructible, it endured years of pinning and buckets of sweat.

I am not, I assure you, the fastest runner on the trail. When I'm running as fast as I can, thinking I am really flying, lots of other runners pass me as if I'm standing still. Occasionally they sound like a bus crunching up from behind. I flinch as they pass me quickly, a ten-person running group, speeding along, chatting cheerfully. Others take more time. I can see a shadow or hear their running shoes hitting the gravel as they gain on me and finally leave me behind.

Some passing runners would say, "Nice tag." A few others would ask, "What kind of a race are you in?" I told them, "God's race." Some even slowed their pace to run with me and talk awhile.

However, I mostly talk to the ones I can catch: some of the slower runners— and the walkers. If I can run faster than they are running or walking, I can run or walk their pace and talk with them about Jesus.

I am happy to say that God is working through me on the trail. Before I head out to run, I pray that God will forgive me and cleanse me of sin, that He will set up divine appointments, that He will send the Holy Spirit to open hearts and lives, and that He will guide me to those who are seeking Him. I also claim the promises in His Word:

> *I am telling you these things now while I am still with you. But when the Father sends the Advocate as my representative—that is, the Holy Spirit—he will teach you everything and will remind you of everything I have told you.* (John 14:25–26 NLT)

The following stories show what God does as I run my race—the race He has set before me. I simply show up, prayed up and ready to do His will.

> *Finally, brethren, pray for us, that the word of the Lord may run swiftly and be glorified, just as it is with you.* (2 Thessalonians 3:1 NKJV)

God calls all of us to run His race. Are you running yet? _____

Get away from Me, You, You, You Baptist!

Lady Bird Lake Hike and Bike Trail became my usual place to share the love of Jesus with anyone I could catch at my running pace—either handing out gospel tracts or sharing the LifeWay F.A.I.T.H. outline and scriptures. Though they say Austin is a liberal city—hard ground for sowing God's word—at least 98 percent of the people I have met have been very interested in talking about God. Young and old. Runners and walkers.

Bud was one of the other two percent. Running like a crazy man, he ran up any odd trailside hill and across every bench or picnic table along the way. Tied together with thick lengths of rope, which Bud sometimes held and sometimes left to drag on the ground, two wild-looking, short-sheared chow dogs ran with him. The dogs were filthy from the trail dirt that clung to them after their cool-off dips in the lake.

When I first encountered Bud, I was still working full time, so I only ran on the trail on Saturday mornings. For months, maybe years, when I ran with the "John 3:16 WORLD = YOU" tag on my back, he would pass me from behind, always making a comment, "Hey, Bible thumper," or "Run faster, churchy." One time I kept up with him for half a mile—not up and down the obstacles, of course.

After talking about other stuff, we stopped while the dogs charged into the lake. Leaving a deposit of mud on my leg, they practically knocked me down on their way. Feeling bold while we waited for them, I asked, "So, Bud, do you think you will go to heaven?"

"Get away from me, you, you, you Baptist!" he shouted, holding up two index fingers crossed in front of him. Calling the dogs, he took off running.

I figured that would be the last time he would talk to me, but God kept setting up meetings. Bud would show up at the water fountain in the small park near my car, or we would end up on the curb together, waiting to cross a street. "Did you bring your Bible with you?" he would ask.

Finally, one cold, drizzly Saturday, there weren't many people on the trail. Bud somehow turned up, and we ran a few miles together.

He told me he was a special education teacher, and it turned out that he was in his fifties—way older than I would have guessed from his reckless running style—and he told me a little about the tough life he had led.

"You know I'm embarrassed to be seen running with you," he said.

"Why's that?" I asked, clueless.

Gesturing toward the trail he said, "Your tag shows you're a Jesus freak. What if they think I'm with you?"

So, on the possibility that I might get another chance to talk to him, I decided to leave the tag at home. It was several months before I saw Bud and his dogs again. Not running with his usual gusto, he came up beside me and we slowed to a walk.

"Hi," he said. "Will you pray for me?"

Trying not to appear as shocked as I was, I said, "Of course. What about?"

He told me that he and his wife were having marriage problems.

"Heavenly Father," I prayed, "please give Bud peace, no matter what, and help him work things out with his wife."

As I said "Amen," he and the dirty dogs took off running.

The next time I saw Bud, several more months had elapsed. He only had one dog on the rope.

"Where's your other dog," I asked.

"Jogger's getting too old to run with me," he said. "I wanted to thank you for praying for me that day," he continued. "Things are better with me and my wife. It seems like all I really needed to do was stop smoking dope."

Letting that go, I said, "That's good, but I'm still worried about your eternal situation."

"You know," he said, "I may not be ready to talk about that, but I have to tell you, I really admire and appreciate you for continuing to try. Maybe one day I'll be ready."

As he and the dog disappeared around a bend in the trail, I called after him, "Don't wait too long."

> The Bible says: *But you must not forget this one thing, dear friends: A day is like a thousand years to the Lord, and a thousand years is like a day. The Lord isn't really being slow about his promise, as some people think. No, he is being patient for your sake. He does not want anyone to be destroyed, but wants everyone to repent.* (2 Peter 3:8–9 NLT)

However, not if they resist too long. The Bible also says:

> *God's promise of entering his rest still stands, so we ought to tremble with fear that some of you might fail to experience it. For this good news—that God has prepared this rest—has been announced to us just as it was to them. But it did them no good because they didn't share the faith of those who listened to God. For only we who believe can enter his rest.* (Hebrews 4:1–3 NLT)

Don't be afraid, and don't give up on prayer. Even when they say "NO!" the Holy Spirit can still draw them to Jesus. When was the last time you obeyed the Holy Spirit's lead by lovingly following up or praying with someone who said no?

_____

_____

He Didn't Know How Many Times

I was gaining on the balding man who was running in front of me. The Holy Spirit was leading me to talk to him, so I came up beside him and slowed my pace a little.

"How far you going?" I asked between breaths.

"I'm in the last of three miles," he said.

"Me, too. Mind if I run with you?" I puffed.

"Suit yourself," he huffed.

"I'm Carol," I said. "Who are you?"

"I'm Don," he answered cheerfully. "Nice to meet you."

As we ran and chatted, we agreed that the best thing about being out on the trail was seeing all the birds, squirrels, babies, dogs, and people. He told me he wasn't training for any specific race, just for fitness.

"Me, too," I said. "But I'm curious, are you also training for spiritual fitness?"

"I haven't thought much about it," he answered.

"Well, I have another question," I continued. "What do you think it takes for a person to go to heaven?"

He thought for several strides. Then he said, "I think I've been a pretty good person."

"I've heard that answer from lots of people," I said. "But it's not the answer the Bible gives. Do you mind if I share the Bible's answer?"

"Not at all," he said.

As we covered the next mile in a little over ten minutes, I shared the F.A.I.T.H. outline and scriptures. I told Don the bad news about our sinfulness and the good news about the life, death, and resurrection of Jesus, His payment for our sins. I told him that we have to turn from our ways (repent) and trust Jesus alone for our salvation. Then I asked if he wanted to put his own faith in Jesus.

"I've already done that," he said.

"That's great news!" I said. "We'll be in heaven together. Don't forget that you'll be there because of what Jesus did, not your own works."

We ran several more yards in silence. "My car's parked right up here," he said, slowing to a walk.

"I have one last question," I said. "How many times have you shared your faith in Jesus?"

"I don't know," he said.

"So, you don't know how many times." I said. "Is that because it's too many, or because it's too few?"

Stopping and turning to look at me, he said, "I guess it's too few."

I watched him walk to his car. Then I continued my run, thinking that just a few years before, I would have had to answer, "I don't know," for the same reason as Don. I hadn't experienced the thrill of helping anyone start a personal relationship with Christ.

Now I can truthfully say that I still don't know how many. Because God has allowed me to be in the birthing room with so many new Christians, I've lost track. It was a matter of committing my life to God's work and getting started.

> Paul wrote: *Do you not know that those who run in a race all run, but one receives the prize? Run in such a way that you may obtain it. And everyone who competes for the prize is temperate in all things. Now they do it to obtain a perishable crown, but we for an imperishable crown. Therefore I run thus: not with uncertainty.* (1 Corinthians 9:24–26 NKJV)

Have you started running your race? _____ Have you shared your faith? _____ How many times? _____ If you don't know, is it too many times to count—or too few? _____

Camping under the Congress Avenue Bridge

As my running shoes crunched along on the crushed granite of the hike and bike trail that circles Austin's Lady Bird Lake, I was in the fourth mile of an early-morning, seven-mile run. Sweat had begun to blotch my pink running shirt. I was warmed up, feeling good, and I was cruising.

As the trail took me under the Congress Avenue Bridge, I passed a young man and woman who were packing up their stuff from what appeared to be an overnight campout under the bridge. It was none of my business. I kept running.

"Go back and talk to them," the Holy Spirit said, in the way He sometimes does.

As I sometimes do, I thought, *I'm running here.*

"Go back and talk to them," He repeated.

Well, I thought, *I could give them a tract.* I turned around and walked back to the bridge.

"I'm Carol," I said, handing the man a tract. He studied it for a minute.

"I'm Rick," he said. "And that's Heather."

Then he began to talk about God, to preach a little. While Rick talked, Heather, who was pregnant—very pregnant—listlessly folded the air mattress and gathered up a tiny pump and their other things. I surmised that she was not thrilled about sleeping under the bridge. As Rick talked on, it became clear that he and Heather were not married. He said he was planning to start a cell phone business, and he was determined to make it alone. However, when I asked him if they knew anyone who could help them in the meantime, he actually mentioned a few likely suspects.

Then I changed the subject, saying, "Rick, are you sure you would go to heaven if you died today?"

Even though he had just admitted that he was living in sin with this pregnant young woman, Rick said he was sure he would go to heaven. He said he knew it was what Christ had done for him, not anything he had done.

"We plan to get married, you know," he added.

I asked Heather if she thought she would go to heaven.

"I don't want to talk about it!" she snapped.

Rick and I continued our discussion about God while Heather refolded all of their clothes and shoved them into a big duffle bag.

Eventually, I asked her my question about heaven again.

"I'm not sure," she said, picking ants off their blanket.

"Well, have you ever heard the good news about Jesus," I asked.

"No," she answered.

"Would you like to know what the Bible says about going to heaven?" I asked. Nodding, she sat down on the duffle bag and looked at me.

Most folks need a bathroom right after they get up—especially pregnant ones. But she wasn't in a hurry to get rid of me. Instead, she listened carefully as I went through the F.A.I.T.H. scriptures.

When I finished the last verse, I asked her if she would like to pray, right there under the Congress Avenue Bridge, to profess her faith in Jesus.

Just as intensely as she had said she didn't want to talk about it, she said, "Yes!"

So, with runners, walkers, and bicyclists passing on the trail just a few yards away, the three of us stood hand-in-hand in a circle. As Heather prayed with me to turn from her sins and accept Jesus as her personal Lord and Savior, Rick said each word with her, rededicating his life.

Thanking me and waving goodbye, they picked up their duffle bag and headed off to find a bathroom—and to begin their new lives. And I restarted my run. After an hour-long, God-sized cool down, I was on fire with the kind of joy only someone who has just been in the "birthing room" when someone is born into the kingdom of God can feel.

> *"Therefore, since we are surrounded by such a huge crowd of witnesses to the life of faith, let us strip off every weight that slows us down, especially the sin that so easily trips us up. And let us run with endurance the race God has set before us. We do this by keeping our eyes on Jesus, the champion who initiates and perfects our faith."* (Hebrews 12:1–2 NLT)

Have you experienced that joy? _____ Write a little note here; then write a story about it and email it to me at cwrite4jesus@aol. com.

_____

_____

He Talked to Me First

Quitting my full-time job to pursue writing, to help Chuck with his art career, and to be more involved in prison ministry also freed me up to run any day of the week. That's how I happened to be running on Austin's Lady Bird Lake Hike and Bike Trail one Monday morning. As usual, I gave my running time to God and asked Him to give me someone to talk to about Jesus.

"The one who talks to you first," the Holy Spirit said.

That seems unlikely, I said to myself. After all, I usually say "Hi" or "Good Morning" to almost everyone I encounter on the trail, but not too many runners or walkers speak to me first. In fact, it's a rare occurrence. Most of them say "Hi" back. But focused on running or walking, on iPod music, or on conversations with running or walking partners, they're unlikely to say it first.

All the same, I was in the first mile of the five-mile loop I was running that day when it happened.

I had stopped for a drink at a trailside water fountain, and a man with two fluffy sheltie dogs came up behind me. "Where's your tag?" he asked.

I wasn't wearing my John 3:16 tag, but I had on a race logo t-shirt. I didn't know if he was teasing me because I was the geek who was wearing that shirt, if he was seriously asking if I was in a race, or if he was wondering what happened to my other tag.

"I don't have one today," I answered, wiping water off my chin with my shirtsleeve.

He was friendly enough, and we took off running together. The shelties trotted along on his other side. After maybe half a mile of general conversation about his dogs and running, I asked him if he would go to heaven if he died that day.

He didn't answer.

The pause lasted all the way across the Congress Avenue Bridge. Then I asked him another safe question about running as we walked down the stairs leading back to the trail on the other side of the narrow lake.

We resumed our running pace and I returned to God's assignment. "Seriously," I said, "if you died today, where would you go?"

"Hell," he said.

I stopped in midstride. Most people say heaven, even if they don't know why.

"Really?" I asked, catching up with him and the dogs again. "Would you like to know how you can make sure it's heaven, according to the Bible?"

"I don't know...," he began, hesitating.

"I can tell you in the next mile or so," I said quickly, "and you can stop me any time."

"Okay, go ahead," he said.

"The Bible says it's all based on faith," I said. "You can spell it on one hand: F.A.I.T.H."

Then, as we ran, I shared the F.A.I.T.H. scriptures, which have somehow stuck in my gray-haired head, ending with the H, which stands for heaven. "Finally," I said, "it all boils down to taking a big step of F.A.I.T.H., Forsaking All, I Trust Him."

"Would you like to pray to invite Jesus into your life right now, right here on the trail?" I asked.

"Yes!" he answered right away.

Again, I stopped in midstride. He and the dogs stopped, too. Ignoring the other walkers and runners, we moved to the side of the trail, bowed our heads and prayed together as he expressed his faith in Jesus alone for his salvation and asked Jesus to take over his life.

"You are a brand new baby Christian," I said, raising my head to look at him. "Just like babies need food and have to learn how to walk and talk, you'll need to grow up spiritually. You can do that by talking to God every day, going to church, and reading your Bible."

"I'll have to get one," he said.

"That's right," I said. "The best place to start reading is in the book of John. The New Testament starts out with Mathew, Mark, Luke, and then John. This will help you learn more about Jesus from the perspective of John, the man who called himself "the disciple Jesus loved." Then read Acts to see what happened after Jesus left the disciples and returned to heaven, and read Romans to see what you should do. Then start with Matthew and read the rest of the New Testament. After you finish that, read the Old Testament and see how the history and prophesies lead right up to Jesus. I also hope you'll come to our church. Here's a tract with the address on it. You'll also find the scriptures we just talked about"

"I can't believe you came to me today. Today of all days!" he said. "I can't thank you enough!"

"Well, you're welcome," I said. "But God set this whole thing up. I just showed up, ready and willing to tell His good news. Thank Him for doing all the work."

> *Through Christ, God has given us the privilege and authority as apostles to tell Gentiles everywhere what God has done for them, so that they will believe and obey him, bringing glory to his name.* (Romans 1:5 NLT)

Folks are waiting for you to show up and tell them about Jesus. Will you do it? _____

Two Michaels

Two young men and I started out that day, having no idea what God had in store for us.

Gray-headed, one-hundred-ten-pound, and five-foot-nothing, I left our apartment a little late. During Austin's hot summer, I always plan to get up early and make it to the running trail before seven. I love the first morning light and the last remnants of cool air.

These days, since I retired from a nine-to-five job, I don't have to wait until Saturday to run. I can run any day I please. I also have the luxury of staying in bed, praying and listening to the pastors on the radio, and taking my sweet time getting up. Then I do my daily exercise routine (stretches, pushups, dips, and abdominal crunches that keep my muscles toned) and I talk myself into —or out of—running.

On this particular Wednesday in late August, I finished my exercises and talked myself into running. To show how precisely God timed the day's outcome, here are the particulars of my preparation. It had everything to do with Him.

On the three-mile drive to the Lady Bird Lake Hike and Bike Trail, I munched on a banana and sipped some water. Arriving at a few minutes after nine, I tucked my car keys, driver's license, and folded gospel tracts (eight English and four Spanish) into the pocket of my faded navy-blue nylon ball cap. Grabbing a plastic water bottle, and touching my hat pocket again to make sure I had those car keys and tracts, I closed the car door. With one hand on the white back fender of my car, I stretched my legs. Then I walked down the paved ramp to the trail that outlines the narrow lake that snakes through the center of Austin. The air held no hint of cool. *Oh, well,* I thought.

As usual, I asked God to lead me to someone He wanted me to talk to. Then I picked a direction and took off running. My pace is slow to medium. Lots of people pass me, but I also overtake a lot of others—probably hundreds on a given day—who are running slower than I am, or walking. If someone is going slower than my comfortable pace, I can actually talk and run, or I can talk and walk. As usual, I passed a bunch of people.

I can't explain how I know which ones God wants me to talk to, but He lets me know. Sometimes, I try to shake off His urging, thinking, *None of these people want to talk to me.* But then the Holy Spirit makes the suggestion even more compelling. As I obediently answer His calls, I experience the joy I would have missed if I had skipped those appointments.

Planning to run the trail's three-mile loop, I had started out westbound on the south side of the lake near the Pfluger Pedestrian Bridge. A mile and a half later, I crossed the MoPac Pedestrian Bridge (which is stacked right under the MoPac freeway bridge). Handing out several tracts along the way, I eventually ended up running eastbound on the north side of the lake. I had passed the docks of the Texas Rowing Center and was almost back to the Pfluger Bridge when I noticed a young man, who appeared to be school age, walking the opposite way.

The Holy Spirit said, *"Talk to him."* Again, I can't explain how He says it. He just does.

I turned around and came up beside the young man, saying, "I'm Carol."

"I'm Michael," he said.

"Are you missing school?" I asked.

As soon the words came out, I said to myself, *Even though it's a school day, that was a dumb way to start a conversation,* but he said, "No, I was going to college. But I had to quit, couldn't afford it."

We did a little more small talk, something about how expensive college can be and what he had been studying, but I didn't wait long before I asked him, "So, Michael, where would you go if you died today?"

We walked several yards while he considered his answer. "I don't know," he finally said. "I haven't really thought about it."

"Would you like to know what the Bible says?" I asked. "I could tell you in the next mile or so."

"I don't know," he said again.

"Well, I'll start. If you don't want to hear it, say so, and I'll stop," I said.

"Okay," he said.

We continued walking. And using the F.A.I.T.H. outline and scriptures, I explained to him that we all need forgiveness because we have all sinned and fallen short of God's glory, but that forgiveness is available to everyone. "After all," I continued, "the Bible says, *For God so loved the world that He gave His only Son, that whoever believes in Him should not perish, but have everlasting life.*' Have you ever heard that scripture?" I asked.

"No," he said. "I haven't been to church much."

I recited the verse again and asked, "Who do you think 'the world' is?"

"Everybody," he said.

"That's right," I said, "God loves everybody. And He loves you. So, then who is 'whoever'?"

"Anybody?" he said.

"Right again," I said. "Anybody can include you."

"Right," he said.

I continued to tell him that, though forgiveness is available to everyone, it isn't automatic because it's impossible for God to allow sin into heaven.

"And that takes us to the T," I continued. "The T stands for turn. If we were going down the road, and suddenly noticed we were on the wrong road, what would we have to do?"

"Turn around and go back to the right road," he answered.

"Exactly," I said. "We would have to make a U-turn and get on the right road. God wants us to do the same thing about our sins, turn away from the wrong road and get on the right road. The Bible uses the word repent. More literally, it means change your mind."

He was still listening, so I continued. "Jesus said, *Unless you repent, you shall all likewise perish.*' He said this to some people who came running up to Him.

They started carrying on about some people who had died when a building collapsed on them, asking Jesus who had sinned to cause their deaths. Jesus didn't even mention those people who had died. But in His usual way, He spoke directly to the people who were standing there, *'Unless YOU repent, YOU will all likewise perish.'*

"The Bible says, *'Christ died for our sins, according to the Scriptures, and He was buried, and on the third day He rose again, also according to the Scriptures.'*

"Jesus changed the lives of His disciples—big time. After all, Peter had denied Jesus. And most of the other disciples apparently scattered when Jesus was crucified. The Bible only mentions that His disciple John, His mother Mary, and a few other followers stayed nearby. The rest of the disciples bailed out on Him, probably afraid they might get the same thing.

"However, they all gathered in a room a few days later, possibly discussing what to do next. Maybe they would go back to fishing or tax collecting. In fear, they had locked the door against anyone who might accuse or arrest them. But suddenly the risen Jesus was in the room! After that, He appeared to them several times, and He appeared to at least five hundred others. Then He rose into heaven, right in front of the disciples' eyes.

"After that, those same guys went from running and hiding to boldly telling everyone about the risen Jesus. Most of them died as martyrs. Peter—who, when Jesus was on trial prior to His crucifixion, had denied he even knew Him—was crucified upside down. Only John lived to be an old man, but because he continued to preach about Jesus, he spent a lot of time in gross dungeons and in exile.

"You have to agree that they had a life-changing experience when they saw the risen Jesus. After that, they were willing to die for the truth they had seen. They made a serious U-turn."

I paused and looked at Michael as we walked. "They definitely did," he agreed.

"So, when we turn from our sins, or repent," I continued, "where do we turn? We turn to someone, Jesus. The Bible says *'If you confess with your mouth that Jesus is Lord* [meaning Lord of your life], *and if you believe in your heart that God has raised Him* [Jesus] *from the dead* [just as those disciples did], *you will be saved.'*

"What does it mean to confess?" I asked.

"I guess it means to admit," he said.

"Right," I said. "We have to admit or agree that we want Jesus to be the Lord of our lives. If we do that, and if we turn from our sins and we believe Jesus died to pay for our sins and God raised Jesus from the dead, we come to the H, which stands for heaven."

I paused to look at Michael as we walked. "Go on," he said.

"Heaven is eternal life with God," I continued, "a new life that starts right here. Jesus said, *'I came that they might have life, and have it more abundantly.'* This means that He wants us to have a joyful life right now. Heaven is also the hereafter, after you die. When Jesus left the disciples, He also said, *'And if I go and prepare a place for you, I will come again and receive you to Myself; that where I am, there you may be also.'*

"Would you like to be sure you are going to heaven?" I asked.

Without hesitation, Michael answered, "Yes."

"You can," I said. "It's a matter of committing your life to God, admitting that you are a sinner and that you believe Jesus died to pay the death penalty for your sins and He rose again, asking for His forgiveness, making Him Lord of your life, and asking Him to make you the person He wants you to be."

We walked several yards in silence. I'm always afraid people will miss this opportunity to open the door of their lives to Christ's knock, maybe missing it forever. But Michael stopped and asked, "How do I do that?"

"We could pray together right now if you like," I offered. "Would you like to do it now?"

He nodded and moved to a shady spot, out of the trail's steam of walkers, runners, babies, dogs, and bikes.

"Okay," I said, "I'll pray a little bit at a time, and you just repeat after me."

Right there beside the trail, we prayed together, and this young man started his new life with Jesus.

Michael looked up and said, "I am so happy you came along today. I was just at a point where I was trying to find direction for my life. And now I have a direction!"

"This is your new birthday," I said as we started walking again, "your spiritual birthday. To be fed spiritually so you'll grow in your relationship with Christ, you'll need to read your Bible. Do you have a Bible?"

He said he didn't have one, so I suggested that, to start with, he might get a New Testament and begin by reading the book of John.

"The book of John starts out, *'In the beginning was the Word,'*" I said, "and a few verses later it says, *'and the Word became flesh and dwelt among us.'* This is a little confusing to some people. Just remember, the 'Word' is Jesus, and it will make sense.

"You'll also need to pray every day—talk to God. And you'll need to find a good, Bible-teaching church," I added, giving him one of the last tracts from the pocket in my hat. "This has the information about my church on the back, and it has the scriptures we just talked about."

He stopped. "Here's where I parked," he said. "Thanks again."

We shook hands, and I watched him walk away. Then I returned to my run, heading back in the direction I had been running originally. I had run only a few yards, however, when the Holy Spirit pointed out another young man.

This guy looked even younger. *Surely he's ditching school,* I thought. But something about the way he slumped on the limestone wall near the MoPac Bridge, his dirty clothes, and the backpack beside him made me think he might even be homeless. The Holy Spirit said, *"Talk to him."*

Obediently, I walked over and asked this kid the very same question, "Are you missing school?"

"No," he answered. "I'm twenty-five, already out of school."

"Would you walk with me for a while?" I asked.

He nodded, got up, shouldered his backpack, and joined me on the trail. Not wasting any time on chitchat I asked him straight out, "If you died today, would you go to heaven or hell?"

He answered quickly, "Probably hell."

"Why's that?" I asked.

"My life," he mumbled.

"Would you like to know how you could be sure you would go to heaven?" I asked.

"Sure," he said.

"I'm Carol," I said. "What's your name?"

"It's Michael," he said.

Isn't that just like God to give me two young men named Michael that day?

Hearing myself say almost the same things I had just said to the other Michael, I went through the F.A.I.T.H. scriptures. He listened and we walked. When I asked if he had ever prayed to make Christ his personal savior, he said, "Yes, I have."

"When was that?" I asked.

"When I was about twelve," he answered.

"Have you gotten off God's track?" I asked.

"I guess so," he said.

"Well," I said, "is it time to rededicate your life to Christ?"

"Yes," he said, "it's time."

As we walked along the trail, I said a prayer of rededication to Christ, and he prayed each phrase after me.

Then he stopped walking and said, "Thanks! I really feel better."

"Has your mom been praying for you?" I asked.

"I guess so," he said.

"Would you do me a big favor?" I asked. "Would you tell her what you did today?"

"Yes," he said. "I'll do that."

With his shoulders back and hope lighting his face, the second Michael gave me a quick hug and thanked me again. He turned toward the bridge where we had met, and I went back to my run, praising God for allowing me to be a part of His work in these two Michaels' lives. I had a grin on my face that probably made the other runners and walkers think I was nuts. I couldn't help it. It's just too much fun to serve our God.

> *It was right that we should make merry and be glad, for your brother was dead and is alive again, and was lost and is found.* (Luke 15:32 NKJV)

Are you available when God sends you a Michael or two?_____
Why?

_____

_____

Racing against Time

Michael Lewis, my former pastor at Great Hills Baptist Church, likes working for God. His administrative assistant told me, "He signs up for everything!" He signed up to be on boards. He signed up to teach other pastors how to lead F.A.I.T.H. Sunday school evangelism. He mentored seminary students.

And Pastor signed up to sponsor a race, "The Race against Time."

He announced the race to more than a hundred three-person F.A.I.T.H. teams gathered at the church on a Monday night: "We are sponsoring a 5K race—that's 3.1 miles—in November. How many of you are runners?"

I raised my hand.

Pastor explained that proceeds from the race would go to help people impacted by the AIDS epidemic in Africa, but our other mission in the race would be to tell as many people as possible the good news about Jesus.

I registered for the race right away, and a few months later, I got up early on a November Saturday. "This race is Yours, Lord," I prayed. "Please lead me to people along the way."

However, as I tugged on my black running tights and slipped my t-shirt over my head, I thought about my last race a few years earlier, the Austin Capitol 10,000. In that race, at age fifty-three, I had trained hard, and I had run the 6.2 miles in 53.5 minutes. At a pace just over eight and a half minutes a mile, it was a smoking-fast time for me, by far my personal best. However, the woman who won the fifty-to-fifty-four age group had beaten me by ten whole minutes. That day, I had promised myself that I would only go through the struggles of a race if I thought I could win my age group—very unlikely.

I said to myself, *Here I am, fixing to run another race. What am I doing?*

Nevertheless, I put on my socks and running shoes, secured the timing chip into the double bow in my right shoe, and drove across Austin to the church where the race would start. Our church had organized the registration, and the other church was providing the site. Escaping the nippy wind, I ducked into the church gym, where I found runners stretching and volunteers passing out number bibs. Pinning my own number on, and heading back outside to get ready for the start, I bumped right into Pastor Lewis.

I'm sure my mission for the race would have occurred to me—eventually. Right after he greeted me, however, Pastor put me on course, saying, "Carol, there's a woman police officer outside. Would you share F.A.I.T.H. with her?"

Walking outside, I saw the officer. Dressed in a black uniform with gold badge and buttons, she was sipping coffee out of a Styrofoam cup and chatting with a huddle of other officers. I couldn't bring myself to interrupt all of them.

I looked around and noticed another officer about five yards away from the group. All by himself, he appeared to be hanging out, waiting for his time to report for duty on the racecourse.

I walked across the grass to him. "Hi," I said. "My name is Carol."

"I'm Scott," he said.

I had no idea how long we might have, so I got right to the point, asking, "In your personal opinion, what do you understand that it takes for a person to go to heaven?"

"I honestly don't know," he answered.

"Would you mind if I tell you the Bible's answer to that question?" I asked.

"Okay," he said.

For the next ten or fifteen minutes, I shared the F.A.I.T.H. scriptures. Scott listened. When I asked if he would like to accept God's gift by making Jesus his Lord and Savior, he simply said, "Yes."

Repeating each phrase after me, he prayed the salvation prayer. After we said "Amen," I told him he should begin his new relationship with God by finding a Bible-preaching church, praying and reading the Bible every day, and telling someone else about Jesus.

As Scott nodded, a superior officer walked up to him, saying, "Go ahead and take your position."

I praised God for the salvation, and I rededicated the race to Him. A dance of joy became my race warm up as I joined about three hundred other runners at the start line.

At the blast of a canned-air horn, we took off running. The racecourse seemed to be all up hill and into a stiff, cold wind as it wound through a residential neighborhood. At first, I could hear Pastor Lewis' enthusiastic voice not far behind me. Though he was at least fifteen years younger than I was, I figured he hadn't trained much for the race. Sure enough, his voice faded after maybe a quarter of a mile, and as the runners spread out more, I somehow ended up in a big gap, running alone.

This is going to be a long three miles, I said to myself.

The good thing was that I could focus my attention on God's work. I started handing out gospel tracts to the spectators. I gave one to a ten-year-old boy who had climbed a tree for a better vantage point, and I crossed a street to run through a front yard and gave some to folks who were sitting in lawn chairs drinking coffee, watching the racers go by. Soon I gave away the last tract, and I went back to running my race. *Even if I hurry, there's no way this pace will win the Race against Time,* I thought.

I noticed that we had gradually turned and were finally going the other direction toward the finish line. It seemed like we were still running uphill and against the wind, but I finally found someone to talk to.

Catching up with a blonde girl who appeared to be about fourteen, I said, "Hi, I'm Carol."

"I'm Jillian," she said.

"How are you doing?" I asked.

"I'm beating my brother," she answered, laughing. "That's him back there."

"Way to go!" I said. Then I got right to the point. "I have a question for you," I said. "If you died today, would you go to heaven?"

She didn't hesitate. "I probably wouldn't go to heaven. I've been pretty bad lately."

I was stunned. She appeared to be a sweet girl who would simply mind her parents.

"Would you like to know how you could be sure you are going to heaven?" I asked. "I can explain it to you before we finish the race."

"Okay," she said.

Running the last mile with Jillian, I went through F.A.I.T.H. again, this time in a halting rhythm between breaths.

As we rounded a corner and the finish line came into view, I asked her if she believed Jesus died for her sins and rose again and if she wanted to make Him Lord of her life.

"Yes I do!" she said.

We only had about fifty yards to go. So I said, "Let's finish the race as fast as we can, and we'll pray after we cross the finish line."

She took off. And putting together my own best kick, I was right behind her.

Then, standing in the street beyond the finish line, Jillian prayed each phrase after me, agreeing that she had sinned and needed a Savior, that He died for her sins, and that He rose again, and asking Jesus to forgive her sins, to come into her life, and to make her the person He wants her to be.

She looked up at me with tears spilling down her cheeks and said, "Thanks for sharing that with me."

"It was all God's doing," I said. "Let's tell your mom and dad."

We found them and told them the news. They all jumped up and down and hugged each other—even her brother.

I walked stiffly to the area where volunteers were giving out snacks and water. If I hadn't been so tired, I would have been dancing with joy again. Instead, I grabbed a bottle of water. As I drank it, walking out the kinks, I noticed that paper printouts of the race results (gathered from computer chips we had tied into our shoelaces) already covered the end of the food trailer.

I wonder how bad my time was, I thought.

Finding my name, I practically fell over. After all that, I had won my age group! The printout confirmed that my time, just over thirty-two minutes for the 3.1 miles, was nowhere near my personal best. But second place had gone to someone whose time made it clear that she must have been walking the whole way. Nobody placed third. *So, we were the only two in the age group,* I said to myself, smiling.

Instead of grabbing my jacket from the church's gym and heading home, I hung around to hear the winners' names announced. Waiting for the last of the stragglers to finish the race, I again encountered Pastor Lewis. He had also finished, and he had recovered enough to point out someone else who might need to hear F.A.I.T.H. This time, it was a young couple pushing a baby stroller.

I walked up to them and said, "Hi, I'm Carol."

They said hello in a friendly enough way. But when I asked them if they knew how a person might go to heaven, the man said, "We aren't interested!" and abruptly turned the stroller and walked away.

However, the man pushing the stroller had finished first in the overall race, so he and his wife were also waiting for the prizes. As Pastor Lewis presented those awards, he included the salvation message in his speech. The young couple heard it after all!

Everyone who placed first, second, or third in each age group won a prize. Pastor called my name, and I went to the platform to collect a coffee cup and a fifteen-dollar gift certificate for a local Tex-Mex restaurant. Then I listened while he called the other names—including Jillian's. She had also placed in her age group.

After Pastor finished, I was standing on the edge of the crowd when an elderly man came up to me.

"Hi, my name is Lorenzo. Congratulations!" he said, holding up his own coffee cup and gift certificate.

"Congratulations to you, too," I said. "What age group did you win?"

"Seventy and over," he said.

"Way to go!" I said, impressed that he could complete the 3.1-mile course. Still on mission, I asked, "So, Lorenzo, if you died today, would you go to heaven?"

He had just heard the salvation message, but he said, "Well, I'm not really sure."

So, for the third joyful time that day, I shared F.A.I.T.H. In a few minutes, Lorenzo had a firmer understanding of the gospel message and was praying with me to accept God's gift of salvation through Jesus. Then I told him to start his brand new life with God by praying, reading the Bible, going to a good church, and telling someone else what Jesus had done for him.

Note: Don't expect your pastor to be the only one leading folks to Jesus. They may just tune that pastor out and need your personal touch.

I found my jacket in the gym and skipped back to my car, forgetting all about being tired. Then it hit me: This Race against Time wasn't about my finishing time in a running race. We are all racing against the time others have left to accept God's gift of salvation. And we are racing against the time we have left to share it.

***

If these three celebrations weren't enough, God arranged yet another divine appointment. Several weeks later, I met a lady named Sally at a Christian women's event. As we talked, it came out that she attends the church where the race was held. I told her about the race, including the salvations. When I got to the part about the police officer, Scott, Sally interrupted me. "Wait, I have to tell you this! I know Scott. He got baptized, joined our church, and he comes all the time."

It's so much fun to watch God work!

> For "Everyone who calls on the name of the Lord will be saved." But how can they call on him to save them unless they believe in him? And how can they believe in him if they have never heard about him? And how can they hear about him unless someone tells them? And how will anyone go and tell them without being sent? That is why the Scriptures say, "How beautiful are the feet of messengers who bring good news!" (Romans 10:14–15 NLT) (Also Isaiah 52:7)

What a joy it is to run in the Lord's race. Time is short. If you haven't already, start your race against time soon, and finish strong. Where will you be running your race?

_____

_____

_____

The God Box

I was running on the north side of the trail around Lady Bird Lake near Austin High School. Passing a young woman who was walking by herself, I handed her a gospel tract from my hat pocket. "This is for you," I said.

"Thanks," she said, taking the folded slip of paper.

I kept running for a hundred yards or so. *Go back and pray with her,* the Holy Spirit said, in a way He regularly does.

I turned and ran back. She was out of sight around a bend, and I was afraid I wouldn't find her again. But there she was, still walking, reading the tract. When I stopped in front of her, she spoke first. "You have no idea how much I needed this today," she said.

"I'm Carol," I said. "God told me to come back and ask if there's anything I can pray with you."

She didn't seem at all surprised by that, and as we walked along, her story gushed out. Her name was Sandra. Her son was four, and something had happened to him. He wasn't injured, but it was something terrible. Beyond the incident itself, the big problem was that he wouldn't talk to her about it.

"Could you pray for God to help him talk to me?" she asked.

We stopped under the dark, thick branches of a pecan tree.

"Dear Lord," I prayed, "you know all about this situation. Please give Sandra and her son your tender loving comfort and healing. Please give her wisdom as a mom, and help him talk to her. We ask this in the holy and powerful name of Jesus."

As I said "Amen," I remembered something I had heard in a prison only a week before. During a Bill Glass Champions for Life prison ministry weekend, one of the inmates had shared with me that she is keeping what she calls her "God Box." Whenever something worries her, she writes it down on a slip of paper and tucks it into her God Box. "That means I'm giving the problem to God," she said, "and I am not to worry about it anymore."

"What if you get your son a God Box?" I asked, explaining the inmate's concept.

"He can't read or write. He's only four," Sandra answered.

"Oh, yeah," I said, thinking as we walked. "Well," I finally said, "what if he uses a rock for each problem. When he puts a rock in his God Box, he can say a prayer and ask God to take care of the problem. Tell him he can tell you anything he wants to about each rock, and you will help him pray. No pressure."

"That's a great idea," Sandra said. Her eyes lit up with the possibility that she and her son might find a way to get through this together, with God's help.

She looked as if she wanted to be alone and think some more. "I'll be praying for you," I said, increasing my pace to finish my run.

> Jesus said: *Again I say to you that if two of you agree on earth concerning anything that they ask, it will be done for them by My Father in heaven. For where two or three are gathered together in My name, I am there in the midst of them.* (Matthew 18:19–20 NKJV)

When you make yourself available for whatever God wants to do in and through you, He will enrich your life, too. When you pray for someone right on the spot, watch what God will do. Will you ask the next person you encounter what you can pray for them? _____

Five Minutes Late, but Right on Time

One warm Saturday morning, in the last half mile of my planned three-mile run on Lady Bird Trail, I noticed a young woman running ahead of me. In His "still small voice," the Holy Spirit said, *"Talk to her."*

"Okay," I said aloud, picking up my pace.

"How far are you going?" I asked, struggling to catch my breath after I was finally running beside her.

"I don't know," she said. "This is my first time on the trail. I'm trying to catch up with my running group."

"I'm Carol," I said, still trying to synchronize my breathing with talking.

"I'm Olivia," she answered.

As we ran right past the place where I had left my car, we talked about her plans to train with a friend. Her friend had suggested that they join a running group so they could run the Capitol 10,000 (a 6.2-mile race on the streets of Austin) in four months. For this first meeting with the group, a series of events had placed her five minutes late, on the wrong side of a bridge, and just a little ahead of me.

Because she was late, she figured the group had started without her. Not knowing which way they had gone, she had headed out, running as fast as she could, hoping she would catch them.

Instead, God and I had caught her.

It took us about a mile to discuss the few details Olivia knew about the training group, and we talked about the 10K race, which I had run a few times before.

As we stopped to get a drink, a man ran by in the opposite direction and said "Hello ladies!" in a much friendlier tone than most runners use on the trail. He and the man who ran with him were quickly out of sight.

Olivia and I looked at each other. "Wasn't that the governor?" she asked, meaning Texas governor, Rick Perry.

"Well, he looks skinnier in a t-shirt, shorts, and a ball cap, but he sure sounded like a politician," I said, laughing. "That guy with him must be his body guard."

"Let's follow him," Olivia said.

He was running a quick pace, faster than we could ever hope to run, but why not turn around and go the same way he was going. After all, I was running beyond the three miles I had planned, my car was in a lot about a mile back, and Olivia had no idea where her training group might be. So, we followed the governor. As you might have guessed, we didn't see him again.

Since Olivia had never run much more than a mile, and I didn't need to run any more miles that day, we decided to walk and talk.

As I often do in conversations with runners and walkers on the trail, I asked her what she thought about God. I had no idea how God had been working in her life.

She replied that, though she had grown up in church, she had turned away from God lately. She told me how her life had become a bad roller-coaster ride.

"But," she continued, "a few years ago, when I was about twenty, God came to me." He had appeared to her in dreams—not once but twice—asking her if she wanted to see Him. She stopped and looked at me.

"I told Him no both times," she said.

As we started walking again, she continued, "Since then, I haven't had another dream about God. I'm sure I've blown my chances to know Him. He'll never ask me again."

"Well," I said, "maybe God was just testing you. After all, in one of the Bible stories [Exodus 33], Moses said he wanted to see God, but God said that Moses shouldn't see His face, that it would surely kill him. But God said He would hide Moses in a cleft in the rocks, and He would pass by, only letting Moses see His back."

At this point in our talking and walking, Olivia's friend and the rest of her training group came along, running in the opposite direction. Until we turned around to follow the governor, we had been about a mile ahead of them.

"I'm sorry I missed you," she told them. "Go ahead with your run, and I'll meet you at the MoPac Bridge."

God is so good! I thought. *That bridge is about a mile from here, so, we have plenty of time to talk. He's removed any concerns Olivia might have had about catching her group, and any worries they might have had her. And she's more interested in talking about Him than joining her friend!*

"Olivia," I went on, trying to keep my voice calm as we resumed our walk, "God wouldn't really let you see Him, and it seems to me that He isn't finished with you yet. After all, He arranged all the details that put us together today. I believe He sent me to tell you the good news about Jesus and how much He loves you."

"Really?" Olivia said, obviously happy about this. "So tell me."

As we walked the last mile, quoting the scriptures that go with the letters in the F.A.I.T.H. outline, I explained to Olivia that we need God's forgiveness, that forgiveness is available to everyone. But forgiveness is not automatic, because we all sin, and it's impossible for God to allow sin in heaven. However, if we agree to turn from our sinful life (repent) and turn to Jesus, trusting Him alone for our salvation and believing He died for our sins and rose again, we receive the gift of heaven, the abundant life here, and eternal life with God in the hereafter.

Olivia listened attentively, asking questions as we walked and answering my questions. We talked about the last scripture as we crossed the MoPac Bridge. Then I asked if she wanted to ask Jesus to come into her life. At that very moment, her running group appeared in front of us.

Olivia could have told me, "Thank you very much," and excused herself to go with them to breakfast. Many people might have done just that, delaying their decision until another time and place.

Instead, she asked the group if they would wait for her. We found a quiet place a few yards away, and she bowed her head and prayed with me to accept Jesus as her own Lord and Savior.

Then we parted. Kicking up my heels as I went, I trotted the mile and a half back to my car—making my total distance seven miles for the day. And Olivia began her new life with Jesus.

Praise God! He allows me the joy of being in His presence when someone like Olivia is searching for His love and forgiveness and finds the life-giving treasure of salvation through Jesus.

When I make myself available to do His work, He uses me. He gives me strength and endurance—even if it means going much farther than I had intended to run or walk, even though I'm just a regular person and a so-so runner. When I simply show up ready to work and listen to His promptings, He lets me participate in His awesome appointments.

He will be very gracious to you at the sound of your cry; when He hears it, He will answer you. And though the Lord gives you the bread of adversity and the water of affliction, yet your teachers will not be moved into a corner anymore, but your eyes shall see your teachers. Your ears shall hear a word behind you, saying, "This is the way, walk in it." (Isaiah 30:21 NKJV)

Jesus said: *My sheep listen to my voice; I know them, and they follow me. I give them eternal life, and they will never perish. No one can snatch them away from me, for my Father has given them to me, and he is more powerful than anyone else. No one can snatch them from the Father's hand. The Father and I are one.* (John 10:27–30 NLT)

When you start your race, you will run across people who are looking for God, afraid they have missed Him. Who have you run across?

_____

_____

_____

Fussing All the Way

In the second mile of my planned three-mile run on a chilly, overcast November Tuesday, I caught up with a young woman pushing a stroller. A white, brown, and black collie trotted along beside her. As they went along, the two-year-old in the stroller was alternately crying and whining at full volume.

I rarely notice little kids fussing on the trail around Lady Bird Lake. They're usually happy to be outside—or sound asleep—with parents wheeling them in strollers along the dirt trail. This one was definitely fussing.

When I see fussy kids in places like grocery stores, doctors' waiting rooms, and airplanes, I usually try to distract them until they forget what they're fussing about.

So, I slowed down to walk with them. The mom's name was Leslie, and her fussy daughter was Shelly. Though Shelly had a Teddy bear, a Sippy Cup of juice, and a soft, yellow blanket, she was not happy. And nothing I said or did made any difference. I told her how cute she looked in her striped stockings, black patent boots, flowered shirt, and little denim skirt. She brightened momentarily, only to start howling again. But her tantrums weren't changing anything. Since the mom, daughter, and dog were a mile or more from their car, Shelly had no choice but to go along for the rest of the ride.

I decided to walk with them. The ice was already broken on my conversation with Leslie, so I asked her, "If you died today, would you go to heaven or hell?"

"I would go to heaven," she answered without hesitation, "because Jesus Christ is my Lord and Savior."

I love it when I hear that answer. "Well, then, what is God doing in your life?" I asked.

"Actually, I'm feeling kind of stuck right now," she answered. "I plan to go to nursing school as soon as my husband and I get the time and finances figured out." The story quickly came out that she wanted to be a nurse so she could take the gospel message to far-away places. Having to wait so long before she would be able to do that was almost unbearable.

I described the ways I share the love of Jesus in prisons and jails across the United States, as well as on the running trail, on front porches, and at gas stations in Austin. I added that many people also go on missions all over the country and all over the world, sharing the gospel without any professional skills.

"Lots of us just tell people about Jesus wherever we are," I said. "We just show up, and God does all the work, equipping us for the jobs He assigns."

The look on Leslie's face changed from discouragement to delight as she turned this over in her mind, even though Shelly continued to carry on with all of her vocal capacity.

As we parted to go to our cars, Leslie said, "I'm glad you came along. I was so down today, and not just because Shelly was fussing. You can't even imagine how much better I feel."

> Paul wrote: *When we get together, I want to encourage you in your faith, but I also want to be encouraged by yours.* (Romans 1:12 NLT)

Who in your day needs your encouragement? A friend? A stranger?

_____

_____

Ken Almost Waited Too Long

Scritch, scritch, huff, scritch, scritch, puff. Scritch, scritch, huff, scritch, scritch, puff. When I met Ken, I was in my Saturday morning running rhythm, circling Lady Bird Lake on the dusty hike and bike trail. I made myself run as fast as I could up a short-but-steep hill toward the railroad tracks where a kid-sized train, the Zilker Eagle, crosses the trail as it loops around Zilker Park. At the top of the hill, an old man and a squatty dachshund were tottering along in the opposite direction.

God said, *"Go talk to him."* So, I turned around.

"How far are you going," I asked, trying to catch my breath.

"Three miles," he answered, as if it were no big deal.

"Wow!" I said, walking along with the man and his dog. Even when I was in my twenties, three miles had seemed like an impossibly long distance to go on foot. And this man had to be pushing eighty.

He told me his name was Ken, and the dog was Heidi. As I said, they were just tottering along. Heidi sniffed every rock, bush, and tree, and Ken waited patiently, moving forward a little at a time. The number of other walkers and runners who stopped to say hello further hindered his progress.

After walking maybe a quarter of a mile with Ken and Heidi, I turned around and resumed my run, thinking: *What a nice man. His little dog and lots of people like him.* At the time, I didn't realize that this nice man was headed for hell.

I saw Ken and walked a little way with him almost every Saturday. It turned out that he walked the three-mile loop every day. And he wasn't almost eighty. He was eighty-eight! Our walk-and-talk friendship on the trail continued for a couple of years.

One Saturday, after I hadn't seen them for several weeks, Ken and Heidi appeared on a different part of the trail, the one-mile loop between the Pfluger Pedestrian Bridge and the Congress Avenue Bridge. He was using a walker, and they were going even slower than usual.

"Hi, Ken," I said. "How are you doing?"

"Well," he said, "I'm not getting around as well as I used to."

I suppose that was obvious.

"I'm moving to an assisted living apartment this week," he continued. "This is my last day on the trail."

I smiled, thinking only God could have timed that last meeting on the trail. Not wanting to end the friendship with Ken just yet, I asked him where he was going. He said something about "Heritage" and "MoPac" (a freeway in Austin). I didn't have any way to write it down, but when I got home, I checked the Yellow Pages and found the phone number. After a few weeks, I called him.

"Hi Ken, it's Carol," I said. "You and I walked on the trail on Saturdays."

"I remember you," he said.

"Would it be okay if I come visit you some time?" I asked.

"Sure, that would be nice," he said.

So, I started visiting Ken about once a month.

Though the exterior and the lobby of the assisted living property wore the plush décor of a resort hotel, his one-room apartment held only a couch, recliner, and bed, with a stove, fridge, and kitchen cabinets in one corner and a wide doorway that led to the bathroom in another.

Ken seemed comfortable, however. On our visits, I would talk, and he would remark, "You don't say." or "Well, isn't that something." The little dog would bark for me to throw her squeaky toys and refuse to give them back after I did. Appearing to be laughing at me, she was our entertainment committee.

Sometimes Ken talked about the people in the photos scattered on the end tables: the two wives he had out-lived, relatives who lived in New Mexico. He told me about his former neighbor, Melinda, who brought him groceries and wrote out the checks for his bills. So, all Ken and Heidi needed was a friend, and that job suited me perfectly.

During our visits, as I hung a few paintings and arranged some knickknacks Ken had retrieved from storage, I learned that Ken had joined the army's horse cavalry in the early 1900s. "My job was following the horses and shoeing them whenever they needed it," he said. "I decided it was too much work, so I transferred to the Air Force—and made a career if it." He laughed at the thought.

In the course of our talks, I asked Ken if he believed in God.

"I never think about it," he answered.

"Well, He loves you," I said.

"It sure is nice of you to stop by," he said.

Arriving at his place a few months later, I found Ken outside, sitting on a shady bench with his new friends, Sue and Roger. We all talked awhile, and I asked if they minded if I shared what the Bible says about how a person gets to heaven.

They said "Okay," so I shared the F.A.I.T.H. gospel message. Sue and Roger sat quietly on the bench, paying close attention. Ken walked off to the side, letting Heidi sniff the bushes. When I asked if any of them would like to pray to invite Jesus into their life, Sue and Roger told me they had already done that.

"It sure is nice of you to stop by," said Ken. But he had heard the good news.

I continued my monthly visits, sometimes throwing Heidi's toys and talking in Ken's apartment. Sometimes we walked Heidi around the grounds. I left with a constant: "God loves you, Ken."

One Sunday afternoon, Chuck joined me for a visit with Ken. Sharing stuff I didn't even know he knew, Chuck asked Ken his reasons for not believing in God and answered each of his questions and doubts with Biblical information.

"You're good, Chuck, very convincing." Ken eventually said.

A year or so passed. One day when I called Ken to make sure it was okay if I came to visit, the receptionist said, "Ken has pneumonia. He's at a skilled nursing facility." Knowing I was a regular visitor, she told me where he was.

On my way up a polished hallway to his room, I barely noticed a little man slumped over in a wheelchair. Ken wasn't in his bed, so I went back to the hall. The little man in the wheelchair was Ken, not the boyish-looking Ken who walked the trail in bright colored shorts and t-shirts, but a frail Ken in a navy blue bathrobe and slippers. He looked every bit of his ninety-one years. However, he asked me to take him outside, so I wheeled him through the double doors and around the outskirts of the property, pointing out God's excellent handiwork on the cheerful sunflowers in a nearby field and on the sparrows singing to us from sapling trees. I left him in his room with the familiar words: "God loves you, Ken."

When I went to see him a few weeks later, Ken wanted to take the same route. This time he walked the whole way. He was balancing on a walker, but walking all the same. I left him with my usual: "Goodbye, Ken, God loves you."

Eventually, Ken recovered enough to return to an assisted living property. His friend Melinda, who had been dog-sitting Heidi, had set them up at a place closer to where she lived and, happily, closer to where I worked, making it easy for me to stop by more often.

The sloping backyard of this hillside property had a flight of stairs with about as many steps as Ken was old. The first time we went outside with Heidi, our little walk took us to the bottom of those stairs. I guess it occurred to me that maybe he couldn't or shouldn't do it, but Ken didn't hesitate. He, Heidi, and I climbed right up. Inside the door to the lobby, we quickly heard that the staff did not want him to try that again. I sternly warned him not to do it, too. He nodded.

A few months later, the receptionist told me Ken was at the nursing facility again. I was afraid he had fallen down all those stairs. But he had suffered a stroke.

This time when I went to see him, he was in bed, practically too weak to move. I helped him sit up and eat his dinner, doing most of the talking, telling him about my work, about things Chuck and I had been doing, leaving him with my usual: "God loves you, Ken."

"It sure is nice of you to stop by," he said.

Ken was a tough old bird. Within a week, he was sitting up in a wheelchair and eating in the dining room. I continued to drop by, helping him eat supper a few nights a week. Though he was on a "liquid" diet, meaning that the kitchen staff pulverized everything from squash to steak into unrecognizable mush, he always finished almost every bite, especially relishing the desserts and the "thickened water," which included sweetened lemon flavoring and cornstarch (to make it easier for Ken to swallow without spilling or choking).

Each time, I stayed until a nurse tucked Ken into bed after dinner; then I left him, saying, "God loves you, Ken."

Though he was eating well, and making his way up and down the hallways in a wheelchair, I could see Ken was failing.

One night, Chuck went with me to the nursing home. When we arrived, Ken was already dozing between the white sheets, covered with a white cotton blanket.

"Hi, Ken," I said softly, putting my hand on his shoulder. He opened his eyes and smiled weakly. "You remember Chuck?" I said. He nodded and shook Chuck's hand. "Do you remember what we told you about Jesus dying to pay for your sins?"

"Yes," he whispered.

"Are you ready to pray to admit your sins, to ask Jesus for His forgiveness, to accept that He died for your sins and rose from the dead, to invite Him into your life?" I asked.

"Yes," Ken breathed in a barely audible voice.

Chuck moved to a spot behind the curtain so Ken and I could have a private moment. But he heard Ken repeat each phrase of the prayer after me, "Heavenly Father, I'm a sinner. I'm sorry for my sins. Jesus, I believe you died for my sins, and rose from the dead. Please forgive me. I make you Lord of my life. Thank you, Jesus. Amen."

My tears dropped onto Ken's pillowcase as I savored that sweet moment. If Chuck hadn't heard it, too, I'm not sure he would have believed how tender and real Ken's commitment was.

It was all about God's timing. In a few days, Ken couldn't even whisper loud enough for me to understand him. "Ken," I told him, "you know something? You're no longer headed for hell. When you get to heaven, remember to thank God. Thank Him that, even after all those years you ignored Him, He has forgiven you because Jesus paid the price for your sins, and you accepted that payment. Thank Him for preparing a special place for you." He nodded.

Not even a week later, Melinda called me at work, saying, "The nursing home just called to tell me Ken's not doing well at all. I hope you can go see him tonight. I'll be there as soon as I can."

I got to Ken's room first. Lying on his back, sheet and cotton blanket tucked under his beard-stubbled chin, he was barely breathing. I could tell he wouldn't be in this world much longer.

"Ken," I whispered, "Don't forget to thank Jesus when you get to heaven." He nodded slightly and tried to tell me something, but even when I put my ear close to his lips, his words evaporated into the air.

I stayed only a few minutes, leaving Melinda to her own time with Ken.

Thirty minutes later, I was walking in the door at home when the phone rang. It was Melinda. "Ken's gone," she said.

With sad and happy tears, I thought about Ken. Until the week before, he had lived almost ninety-two years without inviting Jesus into his life. No one else had ever told him that God loved him so much that He sent His only Son to save him. No one else had ever answered Ken's questions and doubts.

But because God told me to walk and talk with Ken on the trail, and I was willing to do it, and because Chuck and I didn't give up on him, he is in heaven. Even though he almost waited too long.

> *Don't you see how wonderfully kind, tolerant, and patient God is with you? Does this mean nothing to you? Can't you see that his kindness is intended to turn you from your sin?* (Romans 2:4 NLT)

God has a plan. He loves you, and He's patient. But don't wait too long to receive His gift, and don't wait too long to tell someone else.

Are you still waiting? _____ Do you know someone who is still waiting? Write some names here and pray for them.

_____

_____

It Was No Picnic

Austin's Lady Bird Lake Hike and Bike Trail is the best place I've ever run. Its six pedestrian-friendly bridges give me choices of one-and-two-tenths-mile, one-and-a-half-mile, three-mile, four-and-a-half-mile, five-mile, seven-mile, and ten-and-three-tenths-mile loops. The crushed granite trail is a soft surface underfoot, broken only occasionally by short stretches of pavement on sidewalks and bridges. Offering great views of the water and the resident turtles, swans, coots, cormorants, ducks, herons, squirrels, and an occasional snake, the trail goes up and down through the shade of huge pecan, bald cypress, and cottonwood trees.

Except on an occasional dreary, wet, cold day, an endless parade of runners, walkers, bikers, baby strollers, and dogs circles the lake, clad in all manners of running gear, street clothes, Santa Claus hats, antlers, even a giant rabbit suit. My favorites were a mom and a four-year-old girl. Wearing shiny yellow raincoats and hats and black boots, they were singing and skipping in the pouring rain. With all that entertainment, I can run miles and miles, practically oblivious to the distance.

On a sunny Saturday, in the middle of the four-and-a-half-mile loop, I ran up a switchback path that leads to the Congress Avenue Bridge, crossed the bridge northward toward the Texas Capitol, and then headed down some stairs that would take me back to the trail.

Halfway down those steps, which skirt the swimming pool behind the Radisson Hotel, my attention went past the swimming pool and settled on a picnic table I had never noticed before—probably because of all the other distractions.

Three men were sitting at the table. *"Go talk to them,"* the Holy Spirit said.

I didn't hesitate with my usual excuse, *I'm trying to run here,* but walked straight across the grass to the table.

One man sat with both elbows on the table, the second man faced away from the table, smoking a cigarette, and the last man seemed to be sleeping, his head on his arms on the table. They appeared to be hotel staff on a break, so I figured I didn't have much time.

I had already given away all but one of the tracts I carried in the pocket of my hat. I reached up and took the last one out. It was in Spanish. *Help me Lord,* I prayed.

I walked up to the table and said, "Hi, I'm Carol. Does anyone here speak Spanish?"

"I do," one man spoke up. I handed him the tract. He looked it over for a minute and said in English, "Oh, I share my faith with people all the time."

He said his name was Hector. We talked a little about the tract. Then, to make sure what faith he was sharing, I asked him if he thought he would go to heaven if he died that day.

"I'm sure I would," he said.

"Why would God let you in heaven?" I asked.

"Because Jesus Christ is my Lord and Savior," he said.

The man with his head on his arms didn't move. The man nearest to me still sat with his back to the table, taking regular puffs on a cigarette. A little oval patch above his shirt pocket said "Robby." I couldn't tell if he was paying any attention to our conversation, but I asked him, "Robby, what about you? Where would you go if you died today?"

"I don't know," he answered, turning to face me. He put out his cigarette and flipped it into the grass.

"If you want to know," I said, "I can tell you what the Bible says about it in five minutes."

Hector looked at his watch, so I figured their break was almost over. But Robby motioned for me to go on.

Sitting down beside Robby, I quickly went through the F.A.I.T.H. outline. He fixed his eyes on me, listening carefully as I explained that he would need forgiveness, that forgiveness is available to everyone, but not automatic, that it is impossible for God to allow sin into heaven, and that all have sinned and fallen short of God's glory. I explained that, if we turn from our sin and turn to Jesus, who died for us and is risen, we will truly have a place in heaven. I reeled off all of the scriptures, too. It was the smoothest and fastest I had ever explained the gospel.

As I finished, Hector, who had been nodding in agreement, stood up. Break time was over.

"Robby," I continued, "Are you ready to make Christ Lord of your life?"

"Yes," he said, nodding.

I didn't want him to get in trouble for being even a few minutes late getting back to work because of me, so I hesitated. Then the Holy Spirit reminded me, *"Hector just said he shares his faith all the time."*

Hector was halfway across the grassy space between the table and the hotel. I called out to him, "Hector, would you pray the salvation prayer with Robby?"

"Sure!" he said.

"Robby," I said, "I don't want you to get in trouble with your boss. If Hector needs it, he has the prayer on the tract I gave him. It's in Spanish, but he can translate it into English for you. Would you mind praying with him?"

"We're friends," he said. "I'd like that."

As Robby followed Hector back toward the hotel, I glanced at the other man. He had never looked up. Apparently, he really was asleep, or he was avoiding the conversation.

"What about him?" I called after the others. "Won't he be late?"

"I don't know," Robby answered. "He doesn't work with us."

I didn't bother the man. If he wasn't asleep, he heard God's Word, and God's Word doesn't come back empty. If he was asleep, God knows how to reach him.

Walking down the steps toward the trail to finish my run, I gave the job of finishing the work with Robby and the sleeping man to God. He had started it, and He would complete it in His way. If Robby prayed with Hector, then Hector had the joy of being there when a brand new baby Christian was born, and I had the pleasure of telling him the good news.

> Jesus said: *You know the saying, "Four months between planting and harvest." But I say, wake up and look around. The fields are already ripe for harvest. The harvesters are paid good wages, and the fruit they harvest is people brought to eternal life. What joy awaits both the planter and the harvester alike! You know the saying, "One plants and another harvests." And it's true. I sent you to harvest where you didn't plant; others had already done the work, and now you will get to gather the harvest.* (John 4:35–38 NLT)

What about you? Have you also had the pleasure of gathering a harvest or planting some seeds? _____ What planting have you done lately—even the smallest seeds?

_____

_____

Where will you plant today?

_____

She Knew Right Where She Was Going

In the pocket of my cap, I carry my car keys, driver's license, health insurance card, organ donor card, and emergency contact information. I also carry gospel tracts—eight English and four Spanish. I pass out the tracts as I run on Austin's Lady Bird Lake trail.

I sometimes start my run thinking, *I'll never be able to give out all these tracts today.* But, following the Holy Spirit's promptings, I usually do.

Occasionally, however, I return to my car with a few left over, usually Spanish ones, though God also has produced many Spanish speakers on the trail. Two guys turned out to be Spanish pastors! I've given the Spanish tracts to a few people who said they were trying to learn Spanish. Some knew friends who could translate, meaning two at a time will hear the good news about Jesus.

On one Saturday, however, I still had two English tracts left when I finished my run at the paved ramp that leads from the trail to the lot where I parked my car.

As I trotted up the ramp, I encountered two women walking down. I handed them the folded slips of paper, saying, "These are for you."

One of the women took the tract I had given her and walked on down to the trail. The other glanced at the front of hers, no doubt seeing "You Are Invited to Go to Heaven." As if the tiny piece of paper were a rattlesnake, she thrust it back at me, snarling, "I don't want this!"

I shocked myself by saying, "Well, where would you go if you died today?"

Maybe you're wondering why I was so surprised. Well, I often ask this question, but not when somebody is already hostile.

Her answer stunned me.

"Hell!" she yelled, "I'm going to hell!"

Her companion turned around to stare at her, as did several others on the trail.

"I hope you'll reconsider," I said, not knowing what else to say. Continuing up the ramp toward my car, I gave that last tract to someone else, who took it and said, "Thank you."

***

On another Saturday morning, I tried to hand tracts to a group of walkers, and one woman said, "No thanks, you gave us some last week. We talked about them for a whole hour."

"Do y'all want to talk about it now?" I asked.

"No," she answered. So, I ran on down the trail.

Unless God opened the door for me to talk to the people, I don't know what happened next with any of those tracts. I left it to God to finish the work He started.

I did what God asked me to do. Even when I get those rare sharp rejections, I know my actions get people thinking or talking about God, when they might not have thought or talked about Him lately. And I know He's working on them.

But thank God! He has made us his captives and continues to lead us along in Christ's triumphal procession. Now he uses us to spread the knowledge of Christ everywhere, like a sweet perfume. Our lives are a Christ-like fragrance rising up to God. But this fragrance is perceived differently by those who are being saved and by those who are perishing. To those who are perishing, we are a dreadful smell of death and doom. But to those who are being saved, we are a life-giving perfume. (2 Corinthians 2:14 NLT)

You must give them my messages whether they listen or not,…(Ezekiel 2:7 NLT)

Those who heard this said, "Then who in the world can be saved?" He replied, "What is impossible for people is possible with God." (Luke 18:26–27 NLT)

You may be the only one who brings up the subject of Jesus in a person's whole lifetime. Think back over your life. How many people—outside church—have talked to you about Jesus?_____

As you encounter rejections when you talk to people about Jesus, remember this: a person who rejects the good news is rejecting Him, not you. Will you stay in the race—continue the planting and harvesting—even when someone rejects Jesus? _____

Chapter 9

What about You?

As you finish this book, I'm hoping that you won't just say, "I enjoyed this book." I hope you will say, "This book changed my life. I can't wait to tell someone about Jesus!" or "I have already begun to experience the joys of introducing people to Jesus!"

Will you take someone with you to heaven? Anyone who knows Christ personally can introduce somebody else to Him. Andrew introduced Simon (Peter) to Him. Philip introduced Nathanael to Him. Levi the tax collector (also known as Matthew) invited all of his raggedy friends over to meet Him. Philip introduced the Ethiopian eunuch to Him. The woman at the well brought the whole town back to meet Jesus.

> Jesus said: *The seed that fell on good soil represents those who truly hear and understand God's word and produce a harvest of thirty, sixty, or even a hundred times as much as had been planted!* (Matthew 13:23 NLT)

Are you good soil?_____

Bill Fay's instructions about sharing our faith—and Pastor Ed's challenge to do it that very week—compelled Chuck and me to overcome our fear, shaking in our shoes as we were, and introduce our very first person to Jesus.

> *And He said to them, "Go into all the world and preach the gospel to every creature."* (Mark 16:15 NKJV)

I challenge you to introduce somebody to Jesus this week.

Joining the others in the F.A.I.T.H. Sunday School Evangelism programs at Great Hills Baptist Church in Austin, Texas (where we learned so much from Pastor Lewis and the other teachers, and we actually memorized the gospel message) was another giant step in our being bolder in sharing our faith. Because of that experience and encouragement, we actually have God's good news lodged in our heads, and we can tell His awesome message, using His Holy Scriptures, to anybody—anytime.

Standing on all those F.A.I.T.H. night front porches, not knowing who God might lead us to, with the Holy Spirit's power, we overcame our reluctance to "bother somebody." And we conquered our fears about what the person inside that house might do. And, above all, we found the pure joy of watching God work in us and through us.

> *Then He said to His disciples, "The harvest truly is plentiful, but the laborers are few. Therefore pray the Lord of the harvest to send out laborers into His harvest."* (Matthew 9:37–38 NKJV)

Will you be one of the laborers? _____ I double-dog dare you to start memorizing the F.A.I.T.H. outline in Chapter 4 today.

Going to the prisons, jails, and juvenile facilities with the Bill Glass Champions for Life ministry—a ministry Bill Glass calls "evangelism training"—has taken us another giant leap farther along in our walk with God. We simply ask the inmates to read the scriptures on the tract aloud, and they tell us what God's words mean to them. So, we are servers of the Word, not preachers. When we have simply shown up, prayed up and ready to do His work, God has drawn many inmates into His kingdom. He has given them new life.

> Jesus said: *For I was hungry, and you fed me. I was thirsty, and you gave me a drink. I was a stranger, and you invited me into your home. I was naked, and you gave me clothing. I was sick, and you cared for me. I was in prison, and you visited me. Then these righteous ones will reply, "Lord, when did we ever see you hungry and feed you? Or thirsty and give you something to drink? Or a stranger and show you hospitality? Or naked and give you clothing? When did we ever see you sick or in prison and visit you?" And the King will say, "I tell you the truth, when you did it to one of the least of these my brothers and sisters, you were doing it to me!* (Matthew 25:35–40 NLT)

Have you ministered to the "least of these?" _____

Handing out tracts as we go through our daily lives and travels gives us another way to share God's invitation into His kingdom. We experience an unending supply of blessings and surprises as we watch how God works.

The Austin, Texas, *Good News Journal* has a great definition for meek people: "Those who are willing to be used by God. Amazed that God would save them, they are as greatly surprised that God could use them."

It's simple. All you have to do is pray, show up, and listen to and meekly obey the Holy Spirit. Be one of those meek people.

If Paul (one of the most fruitful Christian evangelists of all) said the following of himself, you're in good company when you think you're not up to the task.

> *By God's grace and mighty power, I have been given the privilege of serving him by spreading this good news. Though I am the least deserving of all God's people, he graciously gave me the privilege of telling the Gentiles about the endless treasures available to them in Christ. I was chosen to explain to everyone this mysterious plan that God, the Creator of all things, had kept secret from the beginning.* (Ephesians 3:7–9 NLT)

God knows you are up to it—because He does all the work!

The bonus to all of this joy is the fellowship with Christian brothers and sisters we travel with on our way to homes, apartments, prisons, and jails, and with the Christian brothers and sisters we meet in grocery stores and doctors' offices, on running trails, beside gas pumps, and even in those prisons and jails. Hearing how God is using other people is as exciting as realizing the ways He is using us.

Though we gain such joy, the point remains: This is serious stuff!

Jesus said: *Therefore I said to you that you will die in your sins; for if you do not believe that I am He, you will die in your sins.* (John 8:24 NKJV)

We challenge you to share your faith in Jesus Christ. Introduce someone to your Savior and Lord this week. Ask a few questions about someone's final destination. After all, right this minute, someone you know—or will soon meet—is heading straight for hell!

It doesn't matter how you do it, as long as you make it clear that all have sinned, that God only accepts us into His kingdom 1) when we acknowledge His authority and repent of our sins, 2) when we accept what Jesus has done by paying the penalty for our sins with His death on the cross, and 3) when we believe that He rose again—not because of any good work we could ever do.

When someone says he or she will go to heaven, "Because I'm a good person," I sometimes quote the following scriptures:

For all have sinned and fall short of the glory of God. (Romans 3:23 NKJV)

For by grace you have been saved through faith, and that not of yourselves; it is the gift of God, not of works, lest anyone should boast. For we are His workmanship, created in Christ Jesus for good works, which God prepared beforehand that we should walk in them. (Ephesians 2:8–10 NKJV)

Junior, a godly man in my Sunday school class—known for his sense of humor, but also known for sharing the gospel as he goes along—once said to me, "Carol, you're the woman at the well!"

I wasn't sure whether to thank him or be mad at him. "What do you mean by that?" I asked, laughing. "She didn't have the best reputation, you know."

"It's not that," he said. "Everybody knows the part of the story about Jesus asking the Samaritan woman for a drink, confronting her with her sinful past, and then offering her living water, right?"

I nodded.

"The point most people miss," Junior continued, "is that the woman accepted the living water, believed in Jesus. And right away, she put her water pot down and ran into town to bring everyone back to meet Jesus. She was the first big evangelist. You're like her."

The woman said, "I know the Messiah is coming—the one who is called Christ. When he comes, he will explain everything to us."

Then Jesus told her, "I Am the Messiah!"

Just then his disciples came back. They were shocked to find him talking to a woman, but none of them had the nerve to ask, "What do you want with her?" or "Why are you talking to her?"

The woman left her water jar beside the well and ran back to the village, telling <u>everyone</u>, [emphasis mine] "Come and see a man who told me everything I ever did! Could he possibly be the Messiah?" So the people came streaming from the village to see him. (John 4:25–30 NLT)

The woman at the well must have knocked on every door in town! Are you like her? _____ Will you start today? _____

When I've asked people why God would let them in heaven, some of them—even some people in church—say, "That is personal and private!" Even a woman who answered the phone at a well-known, Bible-teaching radio pastor's contact number gave me that response.

It may make sense for lost people not to want to talk about God. But for those who call themselves Christians—who hold the promise of a home in heaven, and who know the tragedy that people all around them are heading to hell—how can that be? I hope this reluctance is a matter of not being ready to talk about it, rather than being ashamed of Jesus—or not knowing Him at all.

> Here's what Jesus said about it: *For whoever is ashamed of Me and My words, of him the Son of Man will be ashamed when He comes in His own glory, and in His Father's, and of the holy angels.* (Luke 9:26 NKJV)

Do you know Him? _____ If not, the "You are Invited" tract in Chapter 7 will help you start that relationship. If you do know Him, how will you show you are not ashamed of Him?

_____

_____

_____

_____

_____

Others say, "Everyone is going to heaven in their own way." If that were true, why would Jesus have given up His life for us at the early age of thirty-three? He could have lived to take advantage of a much longer ministry. Instead, He willingly returned to Jerusalem, where He knew they would crucify Him.

The amazing thing is that God didn't just give up on this mud ball full of sinners. He didn't have to provide us a way back to Himself at all. But He did provide a way—one way—through Jesus.

> Jesus said: *"I am the way, the truth and the life. No man comes to the Father except by Me."* (John 14:6 NKJV)

When Paul addressed the Sanhedrin, he said: *"Nor is there salvation in any other, for there is no other name under heaven given among men by which we must be saved."* (Acts 4:12 NKJV)

Do you say you are a Christian? Do you believe that you are saved by God's grace from everlasting death (separation from Him to suffer in the place called hell) by trusting in our Lord Jesus alone to save you? _____ Then, like the woman at the well, you simply must tell others about Him.

Although specific methods, words, or training may help build your confidence, you don't need them. You just need to be ready to share the hope you have in Jesus, and the Holy Spirit will provide the boldness and the words. After all, God does all the work. Once you have joined Him in His work, you can become like Paul.

Here's what Luke wrote about him: *Then some Jews arrived from Antioch and Iconium and won the crowds to their side. They stoned Paul and dragged him out of town, thinking he was dead. But as the believers gathered around him, he got up and went back into the town.* (Acts 14:19–20 NLT)

Paul wrote: *But my life is worth nothing to me unless I use it for finishing the work assigned me by the Lord Jesus—the work of telling others the good news about the wonderful grace of God.* (Acts 20:24 NLT)

What a moment it will be when you arrive in heaven and God says to you:

"Well done, good and faithful servant; . . ." (Matthew 25:23 NKJV)

Here are some challenges from God's Word:

But He [Jesus] *answered and said to them, "My mother and My brothers are these who hear the word of God and do it."* (Luke 8:20–22 NKJV) (Emphasis mine)

Thus also faith by itself, if it does not have works, is dead. But someone will say, "You have faith, and I have works." Show me your faith without your works, and I will show you my faith by my works. (James 2:17–18 NKJV) (Emphasis mine)

Jesus said: *I am the vine, you are the branches. He who abides in Me, and I in him, bears much fruit; for without Me you can do nothing. If anyone does not abide in Me, he is cast out as a branch and is withered; and they gather them and throw them into the fire, and they are burned. If you abide in Me, and My words abide in you, you will ask what you desire, and it shall be done for you. By this My Father is glorified, that you bear much fruit; so you will be My disciples.* (John 15:5–8 NKJV)

First, talk to God. This means spending time in prayer every day. Seek His guidance in telling others about Jesus. Ask Him for cleansing forgiveness, divine appointments, boldness, enthusiasm, encouragement, and the light of Christ's love shining in and through you. Ask the Holy Spirit to give you ears to listen and words to say.

Second, enlist as many prayer partners as you can to pray for you every day. Here are a few ways Paul asked believers to pray for him:

Dear brothers and sisters, I urge you in the name of our Lord Jesus Christ to join in my struggle by praying to God for me. Do this because of your love for me, given to you by the Holy Spirit. (Romans 15:30 NLT)

Finally, dear brothers and sisters, we ask you to pray for us. Pray that the Lord's message will spread rapidly and be honored wherever it goes, just as when it came to you. (2 Thessalonians 3:1 NLT)

And pray for me, too. Ask God to give me the right words so I can boldly explain God's mysterious plan that the good news is for Jews and Gentiles alike. I am in chains now, still preaching this message as God's ambassador. So pray that I will keep on speaking boldly for him, as I should. (Ephesians 6:18–20 NLT)

Again, prayer and prayer partners are the keys to watching God work in and through your life. Who will you enlist as prayer partners?

_____

_____

_____

_____

_____

So, now I ask you, dear reader, to pray for us—and for everyone who reads this book—that we will witness God's magnificent harvest through our ongoing commitment and obedience. Here's my prayer for you:

> **Heavenly Father, I pray for these Your chosen messengers, that You would cleanse them with the forgiveness of Jesus, empower them with the Holy Spirit's boldness, and give them the joy of taking part in Your harvest. Make them useful vessels for Your work. I ask this in the holy and powerful name of Jesus. Amen.**

I'll leave you with Paul's prayers for all of us:

> *Every time I think of you, I give thanks to my God. Whenever I pray, I make my requests for all of you with joy, for you have been my partners in spreading the good news about Christ from the time you first heard it until now. And I am certain that God, who began the good work within you, will continue his work until it is finally finished on the day when Christ Jesus returns.* (Philippians 1:3–6 NLT)

> *We also pray that you will be strengthened with all his glorious power so you will have all the endurance and patience you need. May you be filled with joy, always thanking the Father. He has enabled you to share in the inheritance that belongs to his people, who live in the light. For he has rescued us from the kingdom of darkness and transferred us into the Kingdom of his dear Son, who purchased our freedom and forgave our sins.* (Colossians 1:11–14 NLT)

Resources and Contact Information

- Read the **Holy Bible** every chance you get. Steep yourself in the knowledge of God's Word. This one book will answer every question you have about life—here and eternal—and it will help you answer others' questions, as well. Memorize scriptures, meditate on them, and the Holy Spirit will bring them to mind when you need them.

- **Bill Fay's book, *Share Jesus without Fear*,** will help you stop shaking in your shoes. It teaches you how to begin a conversation about God and how to use your marked up Bible to share the gospel. It also walks you through thirty-six ways to respond to common objections. To purchase this book (and for other resources about sharing your faith, including an audio version of "How Can I Share my Faith without an Argument?") visit Bill's Website: **www.sharejesuswithoutfear.org**. You will also find leather-bound New Testaments with his questions and scriptures already marked, as well as those answers to objections in the back—just two dollars each if you purchase a carton of forty-eight. If your pastor would like to invite Bill to speak at your church, he can contact him at **239-939-9642**.

- Contact **Danny Souder of Strategic Mission Partners Global** via email, dsouder3@gmail.com, by phone, **214-394-5250**, or visit his Website, **smpglobal.org**, if you are interested in joining him for **church-planting ministries**.

- If you are eighteen or older, register for a **Bill Glass Champions for Life prison event at www.billglass.org**, or call **972-298-1101**. If you are a former inmate, and want to share your good news with somebody else who needs some good news, you must be released, clean, and off paper for at least a year before you may join this ministry in the prisons and jails. Until then—or if you are a current inmate—start rescuing lost folks and prodigal Christians right where you are.

- **Gospel tracts** offer a format you can easily share with someone. If time doesn't allow sharing, you can give them to people, who can read and understand a straightforward presentation of the good news for themselves. I'll send you the document for the **You Are Invited to Go to Heaven** tract from Chapter 7 if you email me at **cwrite4jesus@aol.com**.

- You can purchase other good gospel tracts from several ministries, including the Champions for Life tract at the Bill Glass Website, **www.billglass.org**. Cru (formerly known as Campus Crusade for Christ) publishes the **"Four Spiritual Laws"** tract, available at **www.campuscrusade.com/catalog**. Another good one is **"Steps to Peace with God,"** a tiny magazine-like booklet provided through the Billy Graham ministries, **www.billygrahambookstore.org**.

- Contact fisherman **Glenn Chappelear's speaking and tract ministry** in care of **The Mitchell Group, Franklin, Tennessee, 877-771-6644**, or at **www.sportsmensoutreach.org**.

- Join **Cru** on a college or university campus near you or at **www.cru.org**.

- **Henry T. Blackaby & Claude V. King's book, *Experiencing God, Knowing and Doing the Will of God*,** will take you through the steps of finding where God is working and joining Him there. For copies of this book, phone **800-458-2772**, visit **www.lifeway.com**, or go to a **LifeWay Christian Store**.

- In his book, ***The Case for Faith*, Lee Strobel,** who was a *Chicago Tribune* legal editor and an atheist before he found a true relationship with God through Jesus Christ, gives his testimony, as well as many answers to hard questions people ask about the Bible and faith. He offers a journalist's diligence by asking straightforward questions of Christian scholars and experts and recording their answers. Visit his Website, **www.leestrobel.com**. Mr. Strobel has also written *The Case for Christ, God's Outrageous Claims, Inside the mind of Unchurched Harry and Mary, What Jesus Would Say,* and others.

- For every-day strengthening of your relationship with God, listen to Christian music and Bible preachers on TV and radio. Listen carefully for meticulous Bible teachers, such as **James MacDonald (www.jamesmacdonald.com)**, **Charles Stanley (www.intouch.org)**, **Chuck Swindoll (www.insight.org)**, and others. Visit **www.christianradio.com** to find your local Christian radio stations.

- Find **Dennis Reinke's** artwork at **www.dennisreinke.com**. Or see images of my husband **Chuck Middlekauff's** work at **www.legacygallery.com** and **www.grandtetongallery.com**.

- Contact the *Good News Journal* by writing to **Editor, P.O. Box 1069, Leander, Texas 78646** or visit **www.goodnewsjournal.net**.

Note: Because things change, by the time you read this book, any email or Website addresses or phone numbers may no longer be valid.

About the Author

Born in Amarillo, Texas, Carol Middlekauff stands five feet tall, 110 pounds, with green eyes, chin-length gray hair, and glasses. Retired from the insurance business, she doesn't really look like a runner, a writer, or someone who might spend time in jail. And she isn't a preacher. She's just an ordinary person. But she and her (also ordinary) husband, Chuck, head out from their home in Austin, Texas, to share their faith as they go along, at the grocery store, on the running trail, by gas pumps, and in prisons and jails across the United States.

Middlekauff graduated with a teaching degree from the University of Texas. And she's an incurable writer and traveler. You may have seen her travel articles in publications such as American Cowboy, New Mexico, and other magazines, or the Dallas Morning News, Kansas City Star, Boston Herald, San Jose Mercury News, New Orleans Picayune, and other newspapers. As she began to write down some of the stories about the amazing things God does as she and her husband share their faith, those stories became a teaching book, *Take Someone with You to Heaven*.

Here's why. Most preachers and pastors tell us to go and do God's Great Commission, but they don't explain just how to do it. So, most Christians don't do it. Middlekauff's prayer is that the stories in this book will encourage you to go and do His Great Commission by showing you how easy it is. It's easy because God does all the work! All you have to do is show up, prayed up and ready to do His will. And just do it.